The Power of Value Selling

Gerard Assey

The Power of Value Selling

By

Gerard Assey

Published by:
Gerard Assey
19/18, Palli Arasan Street
Anna Nagar East
Chennai - 600 102

ISBN: 978-81-971121-4-0

(Image courtesy studiogstock on Freepik: www.Freepik.com-Thank You)

Table of Contents

Preface

Welcome to **'The Power of Value Selling'**- *A Guide to Selling from the Customer's Perspective.* This book is designed to help sales professionals understand the importance of selling value over price and how to effectively communicate the value of their offerings to customers. In today's competitive marketplace, customers are more informed and discerning than ever before. They are looking for solutions that not only meet their needs but also provide additional value and benefits.
The concept of value selling is based on the idea that customers are willing to pay more for a product or service if they perceive it as providing greater value than alternatives. This book will guide you through the key principles of value selling, including understanding customer needs, positioning your offering as a solution to those needs, and demonstrating the return on investment for the customer.

Through real-world examples, actionable strategies, and practical tips, you will learn how to:

- ✓ *Understand the challenges facing today's sales and marketing professionals.*
- ✓ *Define value from the customer's perspective and align your offering with their needs.*
- ✓ *Transition from traditional selling to value selling by focusing on the customer's needs and benefits.*
- ✓ *Build and maintain trust with customers by being honest, transparent, and delivering on promises.*

- ✓ *Effectively prepare for any Sales Call*
- ✓ *Effectively uncover a customer's Needs, Problems and Opportunities and be able to demonstrate how your product features can help a customer meet a need/solve a problem.*
- ✓ *Be able to recommend an appropriate Solution and Close business deals effectively after showing a customer how specific business objectives can be met and benefit by using your recommended product or service*
- ✓ *Use negotiation techniques to achieve win-win outcomes that provide value for both parties.*
- ✓ *Identify up-selling and cross-selling opportunities that add value to the customer's purchase.*
- ✓ *Prioritize the customer's needs and interests. By understanding their challenges and goals and tailor your approach to provide maximum value.*
- ✓ *Shift your focus from competing on price to highlighting the unique value proposition of your offering, as customers are willing to pay more for products or services that provide greater value and benefits.*

So whether you are a seasoned sales professional looking to enhance your skills or someone new to the world of sales, this book will provide you with the tools and knowledge you need to succeed in today's competitive sales environment. By adopting a value-selling mindset and focusing on the customer's needs and benefits, you can build stronger relationships with customers, increase sales, and achieve greater success in your sales career.

We hope you find this book insightful and valuable in your sales journey. Thank you for choosing to embark on this learning adventure with us.

Challenges Facing Today's Sales and Marketing

In today's rapidly evolving sales and marketing landscape, professionals face numerous challenges that can impact their effectiveness and success. Understanding and addressing these challenges is crucial for sales professionals looking to excel in their roles and drive meaningful results for their organizations.

One of the primary challenges facing sales and marketing teams today is the changing nature of customer expectations. Customers are more informed, empowered, and demanding than ever before. They have access to a wealth of information online and expect personalized, relevant interactions with brands. This shift requires sales professionals to adapt their approach and find new ways to engage and add value to their customers.

Another significant challenge is the increasing complexity of the sales process. Sales cycles are becoming longer, and decision-making units within organizations are more diverse, requiring sales professionals to navigate multiple stakeholders and decision-makers. This complexity can lead to delays in closing deals and requires sales professionals to have a deep understanding of their customers' needs and motivations.

Furthermore, sales professionals today face intense competition. The market is saturated with products and services, making it difficult to stand out. Sales professionals must differentiate themselves by focusing on the value they can deliver to customers rather than simply pushing products or services.

Additionally, technological advancements have transformed the sales and marketing landscape. Sales professionals now have access to a plethora of tools and technologies that can streamline their processes and improve their efficiency. However, keeping up with these advancements and leveraging them effectively can be challenging.

Moreover, the COVID-19 pandemic has further disrupted the sales and marketing landscape. The shift to remote work has changed how sales professionals interact with customers and prospects, requiring them to find new ways to build relationships and close deals in a virtual environment.

In conclusion, sales professionals today face a myriad of challenges, from changing customer expectations to increased competition and technological advancements. Understanding and addressing these challenges is essential for sales professionals looking to succeed in today's dynamic sales and marketing landscape.

Understanding Value

Value is a multifaceted concept that lies at the heart of successful sales and marketing efforts. In the context of sales, value can be defined as the perceived benefits that a product or service provides to a customer, relative to its cost. However, value is not limited to just the features and benefits of a product or service; it also encompasses the overall experience and outcomes that a customer derives from their interaction with a brand.

Value can be categorized into two main types: tangible and intangible. Tangible value refers to the concrete benefits that a product or service offers, such as cost savings, increased efficiency, or improved performance. Intangible value, on the other hand, is more subjective and includes factors such as brand reputation, customer service, and emotional appeal.

To understand value from the customer's perspective, it is essential to consider their specific needs, challenges, and priorities. Customers are often looking for solutions that not only meet their functional requirements but also resonate with their values and aspirations. For example, a customer purchasing a luxury car may value the status and prestige associated with the brand as much as the car's performance and features.

Examples

A classic example of value-based selling is Apple's marketing of its products. Apple focuses not just on the features of its devices but also on the lifestyle and image that they represent. By emphasizing design, simplicity, and innovation, Apple has created a strong brand identity that resonates with its customers, allowing it to command premium prices for its products.

Another example is Salesforce, a leading provider of customer relationship management (CRM) software. Salesforce emphasizes the value of its platform in helping businesses improve customer relationships, drive sales, and boost productivity. By demonstrating the tangible benefits of its software, such as increased revenue and efficiency gains, Salesforce has become a trusted partner for businesses worldwide.

Action Plan & Strategies

To effectively sell value to customers, sales professionals can adopt several strategies:

- ✓ Conduct thorough research: Before engaging with a customer, sales professionals should gather as much information as possible about the customer's business, industry, and pain points. This will allow them to tailor their approach and demonstrate how their product or service can address specific needs.
- ✓ Focus on benefits, not features: Rather than simply listing the features of a product or service, sales professionals should emphasize the benefits that customers will experience. For example, instead of highlighting the technical specifications of a software solution, they should focus on how it will improve efficiency and drive business growth.
- ✓ Provide personalized solutions: Every customer is unique, with specific needs and preferences. Sales professionals should take the time to understand each customer's individual requirements and tailor their

solutions accordingly. This personalized approach demonstrates a commitment to delivering value and builds trust with the customer.

- ✓ Build relationships: Successful selling is not just about closing deals; it's about building long-term relationships with customers. Sales professionals should focus on understanding their customers' businesses and becoming trusted advisors who can provide ongoing support and guidance.
- ✓ Measure and demonstrate ROI: To effectively sell value, sales professionals should be able to quantify the return on investment (ROI) that their product or service delivers. This requires a deep understanding of the customer's business metrics and the ability to demonstrate how their offering will positively impact these metrics.

Overall, selling value requires a customer-centric approach that focuses on understanding customer needs, demonstrating the benefits of a product or service, and building long-term relationships. By adopting these strategies, sales professionals can differentiate themselves in a competitive market and drive meaningful results for their customers and their organizations.

Transition to Value Selling

In the dynamic world of sales, the transition from traditional selling to value selling is crucial for sales professionals to stay relevant and competitive. Traditional selling often focuses on pushing products or services based on their features and benefits, without necessarily considering the specific needs and priorities of the customer. Value selling, on the other hand, revolves around understanding the customer's unique challenges and offering tailored solutions that deliver tangible value.

Moving from Traditional Selling vs. Value Selling

Traditional selling typically involves a standardized approach where salespeople present a product or service based on its features and benefits. While this approach may work in some cases, it often fails to address the broader value that the customer is seeking. For example, a customer may be interested in more than just the technical specifications of a product; they may also value factors such as reliability, ease of use, and long-term cost savings.

In contrast, value selling goes beyond the product or service itself and focuses on the outcomes and benefits that the customer will experience. This approach requires salespeople to engage in a deeper dialogue with customers to understand their specific needs and challenges. By uncovering these underlying needs, salespeople can position their offerings as solutions that deliver meaningful value to the customer.

Customers observe that 80% of salespeople focus on value for the seller and only 20% of salespeople focus on value for the customer. This disparity highlights the importance of shifting the focus from selling to serving. Salespeople who prioritize the customer's needs and seek to add value at every stage of the sales process are more likely to build trust and credibility with customers, leading to stronger relationships and increased sales opportunities.

Examples

One example of a company that has successfully transitioned to value selling is IBM. IBM shifted its focus from selling hardware and software products to providing comprehensive solutions that address the specific needs of its customers. By adopting a value-based approach, IBM has been able to differentiate itself in the market and build long-term relationships with its customers.

Another example is Salesforce, which offers a range of CRM solutions designed to help businesses improve customer relationships and drive sales. Salesforce emphasizes the value of its solutions in terms of increased productivity, efficiency, and revenue growth, rather than just the features of its products.

Action Plan & Strategies

To successfully transition to value selling, sales professionals can adopt the following strategies:

- ✓ Understand the customer's business: Take the time to research and understand the customer's industry, challenges, and objectives. This will allow you to tailor your approach and offer solutions that address their specific needs.
- ✓ Focus on the outcomes: Shift the conversation from product features to the outcomes and benefits that the customer will experience.

Highlight how your solution can help the customer achieve their goals and overcome their challenges.

- ✓ Build trust and credibility: Be honest and transparent in your interactions with customers. Focus on building long-term relationships rather than just closing deals.
- ✓ Offer insights and advice: Position yourself as a trusted advisor by offering valuable insights and advice that demonstrate your understanding of the customer's business and industry.
- ✓ Measure and communicate value: Quantify the value that your solution delivers in terms of cost savings, revenue growth, or other relevant metrics. Use case studies and testimonials to illustrate the impact of your solution on other customers.

Overall, the transition to value selling requires a shift in mindset from selling products to delivering solutions that add tangible value to the customer. By focusing on understanding customer needs, building trust, and communicating the value of your solutions, you can successfully make this transition and drive meaningful results for your customers and your business.

The Selling to Value Relationship

At the core of successful sales lies the selling to value relationship, which hinges on the ability of sales professionals to understand and fulfill the needs of their customers. This relationship is not just about selling a product or service but about creating value for the customer and building a long-term partnership based on trust and mutual benefit.

Discovering needs is at the very heart of the selling to value relationship. This process involves more than just identifying the customer's immediate needs; it requires a deep understanding of their business, challenges, and goals. By asking the right questions and actively listening to the customer's responses, sales professionals can uncover underlying needs and opportunities that may not be immediately apparent.

The gap between what buying executives want and what they get is driven by three critical elements:

- ✓ The intention of the salesperson: Sales professionals must approach the selling process with the intention of creating value for the customer rather than simply making a sale. This requires a mindset shift from selling to serving, where the focus is on understanding and meeting the customer's needs.
- ✓ The benefit of creating value for the customer: By focusing on creating value for the customer, sales professionals can differentiate themselves from competitors and build a stronger relationship with the customer. This value can come in many forms, such as cost

savings, increased efficiency, or improved performance.

- ✓ The art of asking the next 'Right' question: Effective questioning is key to uncovering the customer's needs and understanding their unique challenges. By asking right open-ended questions and probing deeper into the customer's responses, sales professionals can gain valuable insights that can help them tailor their solutions to meet the customer's specific needs.

Examples

An example of a company that excels in the Selling to value relationship is Amazon. Amazon has built its business around the concept of customer obsession, where the focus is on understanding and meeting the needs of the customer. By offering a wide range of products, personalized recommendations, and fast, reliable service, Amazon has created a loyal customer base that values the convenience and value it provides.

Action Plan & Strategies

To build and maintain a strong Selling to Value relationship, sales professionals can adopt the following strategies:

- ✓ Focus on understanding the customer: Take the time to research and understand the customer's business, industry, and challenges. This will allow you to tailor your solutions to meet their specific needs.
- ✓ Ask the right questions: Effective questioning is key to uncovering the customer's needs and understanding their priorities. Ask open-ended questions that encourage the customer to share their thoughts and feelings.

- ✓ Listen actively: Pay close attention to the customer's responses and ask follow-up questions to clarify and deepen your understanding. Listening actively shows the customer that you value their input and are committed to finding the right solution for them.
- ✓ Provide value-added solutions: Offer solutions that go beyond the customer's immediate needs and provide additional value. This could include offering bundled services, providing ongoing support, or offering discounts for repeat business.
- ✓ Build trust and credibility: Be honest and transparent in your interactions with customers. Deliver on your promises and always strive to exceed their expectations. Building trust and credibility will strengthen your relationship with the customer and increase the likelihood of repeat business.

By focusing on understanding the customer's needs, asking the right questions, and providing value-added solutions, sales professionals can build strong Selling to Value relationships that drive long-term success for both parties.

Key Attributes of Sales Professionals to be More Customer Value-focused

Here is a list of key attributes a sales professional should develop to be more customer value-focused:

- ✓ **Empathy**: Understanding the customer's perspective, needs, and challenges.
- ✓ **Active Listening**: Paying full attention to the customer's words, tone, and body language.
- ✓ **Curiosity**: Asking insightful questions to uncover the customer's true needs and priorities.
- ✓ **Product Knowledge**: Understanding the features and benefits of the product or service being sold.
- ✓ **Problem-Solving Skills**: Offering creative solutions to meet the customer's needs and address their challenges.
- ✓ **Communication Skills**: Clearly and effectively conveying the value of the product or service to the customer.
- ✓ **Adaptability**: Being flexible and able to adjust your approach based on the customer's feedback and needs.
- ✓ **Resilience**: Maintaining a positive attitude and persistence, especially in the face of rejection or challenges.
- ✓ **Relationship Building**: Building trust and rapport with customers to foster long-term relationships.

- ✓ **Customer Focus**: Making the customer's needs and satisfaction a top priority in all interactions.

Why the Right Attitude and Mindset is Most Important!

In any environment, whether at home or at work, the tendency to think positively and approach each and every task with a "can-do" attitude can be really infectious. Organizations are therefore very careful to have the right kind of people to prevent any potential problems among existing employees, as when it comes to selling or working in a team, the positive attitude can spill over into the way, enabling employees to cooperate with one another. On the other hand, employees with a poor attitude about the market, customers, work and the tasks they are required to complete will have a negative effect on those around them. Just as a positive attitude is infectious and spreads to others, so too will poor attitudes have a negative effect on employee relations, resulting in division in the workplace, making it difficult for employees to collaborate with one another, as the poor attitudes spill over into how they treat one another.

Irrespective of whatever profession or business you are in, you will know that while every business requires C.A.S.H. to survive and succeed....Every Professional also needs something to succeed, which I believe is more valuable than the CASH that comes in. This is 'K.A.S.H.' because only when you have this KASH in you, you will be more successful in bringing in the CASH for you and/or the organization you represent, by ensuring and protecting the credibility and image of the organization.

So what is this KASH?

- ✓ **K**nowledge
- ✓ **A**ttitude
- ✓ **S**kills
- ✓ **H**abits

Knowledge is all about a Company's Products or Services that they offer, the Market and Industry/domain that they operate in, together with knowing of who are the other players or the competition that are in this industry. It also involves knowing where the organization stands against them-their strengths and areas that the competition has an advantage over, along with being thorough on the rates, polices and regulations in the industry and market.

How effectively are you able to transfer any knowledge you possess, to the customer/ others to enable them to deal or decide upon the next step or you as their service provider or vendor is a skill.

Now there are various types of skill sets that people possess-Some examples for skills are:

Interpersonal Skills
Problem Solving Skills
Selling Skills
Networking Skills
Time Management
Team Working
Presentation Skills
Effective Probing Skills
Ability to present thoughts/ product demos
Effective Communication Skills
People Handing Skills/ Inter-personal Skills

Having just Knowledge and Skills alone is not enough. There are many people you probably know of, that have a great bank of knowledge along with the necessary skills, but yet have been total failures. Reason being they had a lousy attitude or very poor habits that killed a potential sale or the potential in them; that ultimately affected theirs and their organizations credibility

What you are seeing on the pie chart is the mental make-up of a Professional. As you will see, 50% has to do with the Attitude, followed by 25% on People Skills. In other words, if you don't have the required knowledge or skills, as you can see, you may be able to still succeed with the right attitude and people skills, because those two account for 75%. Now don't get me wrong, I am not saying that you should not work on your knowledge and skills…Absolutely no!

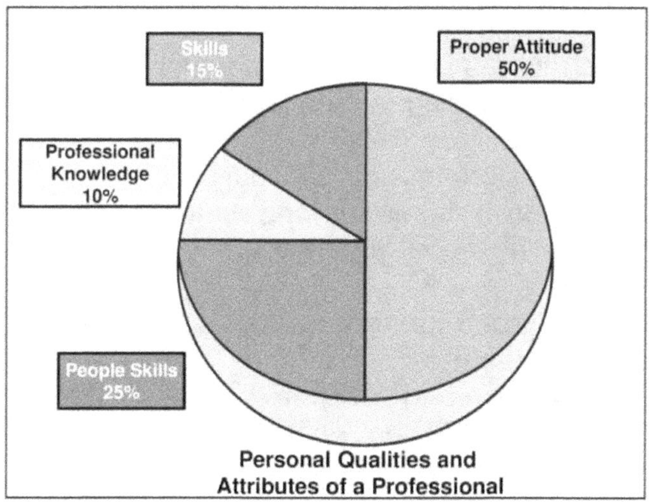

What I am saying is that given that you have the right attitude coupled with the right people skills, knowledge and skills, you don't have to guess where your career graph would be!

Let us look at this a little differently….Assuming you have the right attitude and people skills, which together comprise of 75% but lack the required knowledge and skills, well then, to me, with the right attitude you can easily learn them. And one of the attributes that will pay dividends is someone who has a desire to learn or is teachable, as Knowledge and Skills are teachable, but not Attitude!

Attitude is the outlook or perception towards a given situation, and for any professional, this is extremely crucial and foundational-especially during a downtime! Attitude is made up from our upbringing, environment, exposure etc. It would therefore be very difficult or it would take a long time to undo a wrong attitude that has gone in all these years. And if you are working with other people, like that of sales, customer service or in other departments, then this is very important- as customers remember the wrong or negative attitude longer. You are the only thing the customer sometimes sees of your company- and this is the impression formed of your entire company- good or bad! It takes a long time to undo this negative feeling about your company in the mind of the customer.

At this stage it is important to realize that there are **3 A's of Business life**:

Ability, Ambition and **Attitude**

- ✓ Ability establishes 'what' someone does
- ✓ Ambition determines 'how much' he does
- ✓ But Attitude alone 'guarantees how' he does it!

Ability will bring one a pay cheque (check)

Ambition will get him a raise

Attitude alone will lead to success in everything!

Attitude is actually the 'YOU on the job. When ability and ambition in two people are about equal, how does the boss select one over the other for promotion? Here is where Attitude is the deciding factor. Attitude reflects a little plus- that something extra is given willingly though not required.

If you look at the word A-T-T-I-T-U-D-E itself, is it a mere coincidence that "I" comes first and "U" later? If this has any significance, then in trying to understand the attitudes of people, we should first examine ourselves in relation to other people!

Because Attitude is so very important, this is why it is so crucial to fill our minds with the right positive thoughts (especially when all the world seems flooded with negativity) because our thoughts work into decisions that form our actions and this continued action leads to a habit, which eventually makes up our attitude. Your habits today will become your attitude in the days to come. That's why it is important to check our habits as well. As an example: The habit of being late (at say your office), if not nipped in the early stages can lead it to becoming an attitude, with everything that you undertake being late or delayed!

Here are some examples of positive or right attitude:

Belief
Commitment
Desire
Ability to fail & learn from it
Persistent goals
Self-Motivation
Enthusiasm
Purpose
Self-discipline
Confidence
Creativity
Empathy

Go the extra mile
Self-improvement
Time organization
...and most of all the *PASSION!*

Great Sales Professionals...

- ✓ Understand themselves and how their behavior affects others
- ✓ Have a positive attitude, which reflects in dedication to getting it right the first time, and commitment to helping others
- ✓ Know how to adapt their behavior to meet the differing needs of the situation
- ✓ A willingness to take responsibility
- ✓ Have the confidence to stay calm under pressure

In studies conducted on what makes only a few stand apart as CHAMPION performers, whilst the rest are mediocre, the following was seen as the difference:

Champion Performer	Average Performer
- Plans Questions	- Plans Presentations
- Focuses on large strategic sales	- Focuses on quick hits
- Uses different strategies for different competitors	- Uses one strategy to cover all
- Gets quickly to business	- Spends a lot of time in Preliminary talk
- Asks question with impact	- Asks questions that have less focus and often seem to go nowhere

- Holds back from giving product details early in the sale	- Jumps in early in the sale with product presentations / description
- Doesn't talk about capabilities unless they are important to the customer	- Dumps product features and capabilities on the customer
- Ends the call by agreeing on next steps and joint action plans	- Often ends calls with no actions agreed

Attitude Impacts Outcome

Steps to change your Attitude...

- ✓ Become aware of your negative attitude towards yourself, other people and situations and alter your thinking
- ✓ Think for yourself and become more constructive
- ✓ Keep an open mind

Remember: Changes are always: M.A.D.E...!!!

Developing GREAT Positive Attitudes is not something that happens to you-it is something you make happen...and like any change, it is not easy!

Here are some steps that can help:

M- Mental Pictures: Visualize who you are, what you want, how will you conduct and carry yourself. Formulate and stamp indelibly on your mind a mental picture of yourself as succeeding. Hold this picture tenaciously. Never permit it to fade. Your mind will seek to bring this picture into form.

A- Affirmations: Add a new self-image by talking positively

D- Daily Successes: Build confidence everyday by looking at your positives rather than negatives. Make a true estimate of your own ability, and then raise it 10 percent. Do not become egotistical but develop a wholesome self-respect.

E- Environmental Influences: Do not try to copy or be someone else. Nobody can be you as well as you can. But surround yourself with positive influencers, read positive stuff, listen and watch positive information etc

You are what you think! To change any habits, you must first change any thoughts, feelings and values!

Changing Bad Habits into Good Ones!

Step 1: List your bad habits

Step 2: What were the original causes?

Step 3: What are the supporting causes?

Step 4: Determine a positive habit to replace the bad one.

Step 5: Think about the good habit, its benefits and results.

Step 6: Take action to develop this habit.

Step 7: Daily act upon this habit for reinforcement.

Step 8: Reward yourself by noting one of the benefits from your good habit

Why the Right Attitude and Mindset is Most Important when Selling Value?

The right attitude and mindset are crucial when selling value because they determine how a sales professional approaches their interactions with customers and the level of value they can deliver. Here's why they are most important:

Focus on Customer Needs: The right attitude and mindset help sales professionals focus on understanding and addressing the customer's needs rather than just pushing a product or service. This customer-centric approach is key to selling value.

Building Trust: A positive attitude and mindset build trust with customers, making them more receptive to the sales professional's message. Trust is essential for selling value, as customers need to believe that the product or service will deliver the promised benefits.

Resilience and Persistence: The right attitude and mindset help sales professionals stay resilient and persistent, especially in the face of rejection or challenges. Selling value often requires overcoming objections and obstacles, which requires a positive attitude and determination.

Creativity and Innovation: A positive attitude and mindset encourage creativity and innovation in finding solutions that add value to the customer. Sales professionals with the right mindset are more likely to think outside the box and come up with unique value propositions.

Long-Term Relationships: Selling value is not just about making a sale; it's about building long-term relationships with customers. The right attitude and mindset help sales professionals focus on building these relationships by providing ongoing value and support.

In summary, the right attitude and mindset are crucial when selling value because they shape how sales professionals approach their interactions with customers, their ability to build trust and relationships, and their resilience in overcoming challenges.

Building Trust and Credibility

Building trust and credibility with customers is essential for sales professionals looking to provide value from the customer's perspective. Trust forms the foundation of any successful relationship and is crucial in sales, where customers are often wary of being sold to. Here are some strategies for building trust with customers, emphasizing honesty, transparency, and delivering on promises:

1. **Honesty and Integrity**: Be honest in all your interactions with customers. Avoid exaggerating the benefits of your product or service and be transparent about any limitations or drawbacks. Customers appreciate honesty and are more likely to trust sales professionals who are upfront and truthful.
   Example: Instead of overselling the capabilities of your software, acknowledge its strengths and be transparent about areas where it may not be the best fit for the customer.
2. **Transparency**: Transparency builds trust by showing customers that you have nothing to hide. Provide clear and accurate information about your products or services, pricing, and terms and conditions. Transparency helps customers feel confident in their decision-making process.
   Example: Clearly outline the pricing structure of your product or service, including any additional fees or charges, so that customers know exactly what to expect.

3. **Delivering on Promises**: One of the best ways to build trust is to deliver on your promises. If you make a commitment to a customer, ensure that you follow through and deliver on time and as expected. Consistently delivering on promises helps build credibility and trust over time.
   Example: If you promise a customer a product demo by a certain date, make sure to schedule and conduct the demo as promised, providing a positive experience for the customer.
4. **Active Listening**: Show customers that you value their input by actively listening to their needs and concerns. Repeat back what you've heard to ensure understanding and demonstrate empathy.
   Example: During a sales conversation, listen carefully to the customer's challenges and objectives. Repeat back key points to show that you understand their needs and are committed to finding a solution that meets those needs.
5. **Follow-up and Support**: Provide ongoing support and follow-up after the sale to ensure customer satisfaction. Address any issues or concerns promptly and demonstrate your commitment to customer success.
   Example: After closing a sale, follow up with the customer to ensure that they are satisfied with their purchase and offer any additional support or resources they may need.

Action Plan:

- ✓ Assess Current Practices: Evaluate your current approach to customer interactions to identify areas where you can improve trust and credibility.

- ✓ Training and Development: Provide training to sales teams on the importance of trust and credibility in sales. Include role-playing exercises to practice honest and transparent communication.
- ✓ Establish Clear Policies: Develop clear policies and guidelines for sales professionals to follow, emphasizing honesty, transparency, and delivering on promises.
- ✓ Monitor and Measure: Implement systems to monitor and measure customer trust and satisfaction levels. Use feedback to identify areas for improvement.
- ✓ Continuous Improvement: Continuously seek ways to improve trust and credibility with customers. Solicit feedback from customers and incorporate it into your sales approach.

By implementing these strategies and actions, sales professionals can build trust and credibility with customers, leading to stronger relationships and increased sales opportunities.

Ethical Selling Practices

Ethical behavior in sales is essential for building trust, maintaining long-term relationships, and ensuring customer satisfaction. Ethical sales practices focus on respecting customer boundaries, avoiding manipulative tactics, and prioritizing the best interests of the customer. Here's a detailed exploration of ethical selling practices, including examples and action plans:

1. **Respecting Customer Boundaries**: Ethical sales professionals respect the boundaries and preferences of their customers. This means avoiding aggressive sales tactics and being mindful of how and when they engage with customers.
   Example: Instead of repeatedly contacting a customer who has expressed disinterest, an ethical salesperson respects their decision and moves on to other potential leads.
2. **Transparency and Honesty**: Ethical sales professionals are transparent about their products or services, pricing, and terms. They do not withhold information or use misleading tactics to secure a sale.
   Example: An ethical salesperson clearly explains the features, benefits, and limitations of a product to a customer, ensuring they have all the information needed to make an informed decision.
3. **Avoiding Manipulative Tactics**: Ethical sales professionals do not use manipulative tactics to pressure customers into making a purchase. They focus on understanding the

customer's needs and providing solutions that genuinely benefit them.
Example: Instead of creating false urgency by claiming a product is only available at a discounted price for a limited time, an ethical salesperson focuses on the product's value and how it meets the customer's needs.

4. **Respecting Privacy**: Ethical sales professionals respect customer privacy and confidentiality. They do not share or misuse customer information for personal gain.
Example: An ethical salesperson ensures that customer information is securely stored and only used for legitimate business purposes.
5. **Empathy and Understanding**: Ethical sales professionals approach each customer interaction with empathy and understanding. They listen actively to customer needs and concerns, seeking to provide solutions that address these issues.
Example: An ethical salesperson takes the time to understand a customer's unique challenges and offers personalized solutions that meet their specific needs.

Action Plan:

- ✓ Ethics Training: Provide training to sales teams on ethical selling practices, including examples of ethical and unethical behavior.
- ✓ Ethics Guidelines: Establish clear guidelines and policies regarding ethical behavior in sales. Ensure that all sales professionals understand and adhere to these guidelines.
- ✓ Monitoring and Feedback: Implement systems to monitor sales interactions and provide feedback on ethical behavior. Encourage

open communication and transparency within the sales team.

- ✓ Customer Feedback: Solicit feedback from customers regarding their interactions with sales professionals. Use this feedback to identify any areas for improvement in ethical practices.
- ✓ Continuous Improvement: Continuously review and update your ethical selling practices to ensure they align with evolving customer expectations and industry standards.

By emphasizing ethical behavior in sales and ensuring that all sales professionals adhere to these principles, you can build trust with customers and establish a reputation for integrity and honesty in your sales practices.

The Key: Your Preparation and Research

Effective preparation and research are essential components of successful sales strategies. They enable sales professionals to understand their customers' needs, tailor their approach, and ultimately, increase their chances of closing deals. By investing time and effort into preparation and research, sales professionals can gain valuable insights that will help them build stronger relationships with their customers and drive better outcomes.

Importance of Preparation & Research

Preparation and research are critical for several reasons. Firstly, they allow sales professionals to gain a deeper understanding of their customers' businesses, industries, and challenges. This knowledge enables sales professionals to tailor their solutions to meet the specific needs of each customer, increasing the likelihood of success.

Secondly, preparation and research help sales professionals build credibility with their customers. By demonstrating a thorough understanding of the customer's business and industry, sales professionals can position themselves as trusted advisors who can provide valuable insights and guidance.

Finally, preparation and research enable sales professionals to anticipate and address potential objections or concerns that the customer may have. By proactively addressing these issues, sales professionals can build confidence and trust with their customers, making it easier to close deals.

Research: Analyze Customer Situation, Identify Buying Reasons, Tune In with Customer

Analyzing the customer's situation involves gathering information about their current challenges, goals, and priorities. This information can help sales professionals tailor their solutions to meet the customer's specific needs. Identifying buying reasons involves understanding why the customer is interested in purchasing a particular product or service. This information can help sales professionals position their offerings in a way that resonates with the customer's motivations.

Tuning in with the customer involves actively listening to their needs and concerns. This requires empathy and a willingness to understand the customer's perspective. By tuning in with the customer, sales professionals can build rapport and trust, making it easier to establish a successful relationship.

Research: Market, Industry, Competition

Researching the market, industry, and competition is essential for understanding the broader context in which the customer operates. This information can help sales professionals identify trends, opportunities, and threats that may impact the customer's business. By staying informed about market and industry developments, sales professionals can position themselves as knowledgeable experts who can provide valuable insights and advice.

Understanding the Key Stakeholders

Identifying and understanding the key stakeholders involved in the buying process is crucial for sales professionals. This includes not only the decision-makers but also influencers and gatekeepers who may have a say in the final decision. By understanding the key stakeholders' roles, motivations, and concerns, sales professionals can tailor their approach to effectively engage with each stakeholder and navigate the buying process more effectively.

Asking the Right Questions

Asking the right questions is a critical skill for sales professionals. Effective questioning allows sales professionals to uncover valuable information about the customer's needs, priorities, and challenges. By asking open-ended questions that encourage the customer to share their thoughts and feelings, sales professionals can gain deeper insights that will help them tailor their solutions to meet the customer's specific needs.

Business Needs Identification - The Business Metrics: Strategy, Market, People, Structure, etc.

Identifying the customer's business needs involves understanding their strategic objectives, market position, and organizational structure. This information can help sales professionals tailor their solutions to address the customer's specific business challenges and goals. By aligning their offerings with the customer's business metrics, sales professionals can demonstrate the value of their solutions and increase their chances of success.

Examples

A company that exemplifies the importance of preparation and research is McKinsey & Company, a global management consulting firm. McKinsey is known for its rigorous research and analysis, which forms the basis of its strategic recommendations to clients. By investing heavily in preparation and research, McKinsey is able to provide clients with valuable insights and actionable strategies that drive business growth.

Another example is HubSpot, a leading provider of inbound marketing and sales software. HubSpot conducts extensive research on market trends, customer behavior, and industry best practices, which it shares with its customers through its blog, ebooks, and other content. By providing valuable insights and advice, HubSpot has established itself as a trusted resource for marketers and sales professionals alike.

Action Plan & Strategies

To incorporate preparation and research into their sales strategies, sales professionals can follow these action plans and strategies:

- ✓ Set aside dedicated time for preparation and research: Allocate time in your schedule specifically for researching your customers, their industries, and their competitors. This will ensure that you have the information you need to tailor your approach effectively.
- ✓ Use a variety of sources: Gather information from a variety of sources, including online research, industry reports, and conversations with colleagues and mentors. This will give you a well-rounded view of the customer's business and industry.
- ✓ Develop a research template: Create a template or checklist that you can use to gather and organize information about your customers. This will help ensure that you cover all the essential points and stay organized throughout the research process.
- ✓ Tailor your approach: Use the information you gather through research to tailor your

approach to each customer. This may involve customizing your messaging, offering specific solutions, or addressing particular pain points.

- ✓ Follow up: After your initial research, continue to gather information about your customers and their industries. This will help you stay informed about changes and developments that may impact your sales efforts.

By incorporating these strategies into their sales process, sales professionals can effectively leverage preparation and research to build stronger relationships with their customers and drive better outcomes for their business.

Uncovering Needs, Challenges and Pain Areas

Effective Questioning Skills

As budgets become tighter, competition increases and nice-to-haves are replaced by need-to-haves, it's only the sales people who are willing to take the time to develop strong bonds that will be able to break through. And this step which is the process of uncovering the client' needs, problems, opportunities or pain areas by which can be solved by the products or services of your company can help you to a great extent. When trying to unravel needs, it must be done in a logical pattern that will bring the customer to a stage of realization that there is a problem or need.

So the art of uncovering needs requires the use of different types of questions. First let us have an understanding of the different types of questions that we could ask someone. Though there are several types of questions, for the purpose of this exercise let us look at just the 2 most important ones ie;

OPEN Questions

CLOSED Questions

Depending on what type of answer you want from the other person, either of these questions are used.

Eg; If I asked you: *'Did you have your dinner'?*

Or *'Do you like this training session?'* or *'Are you going home this evening'?*

The only possible answer that you could give me would either be a *'yes'* or a *'no'*

That is why this type of Question is called a 'closed Question', because the only possible answer would be a one word- with either a *'yes'* or *'no'*

Closed questions usually begin with:
'Are you…'
'Will you…'
'Do you…'
'Would you…'
They are usually not very helpful in starting a conversation and extracting information. However, most sales people are more comfortable asking such questions, which we need to avoid at this stage.
The opposite of 'closed' is the obvious: 'open'.
Open questions allow the customer to open up or do the talking and are used to encourage a client to speak freely about a concern or expand on something already raised during the conversation
Always remember this: Open Questions generally begin with 5W's and 1 H ie;
Who?
What?
When?
Where?
Why?
How?
And they encourage the other person to open up and speak.
If we were to redo that example again using open questions, they would go something like this: *'What did you have for dinner?' 'How do you feel about this training?' 'What plans do you have for this evening'?*
These questions will certainly not fetch you a *'yes'* or *'no'* like how closed questions do. But they would allow the other person to open up with information which is what you as a sales person require.
Shooting out these questions without any logical order would also be inappropriate, as it could be unprofessional, could be irritating at times and most

of all cause confusion in the mind of the customer. But if the customer was taken through a logical pattern, it could help lead him or open up to an understanding of his own situation, problem or need-that many times he may not be aware of.

There are two methodologies that could be used. Either of them is fine and would depend on which one you get more comfortable with. We recommend though, that the first method be used for simple, non complicated accounts, whilst the second method be used for complicated or major accounts.

The logical pattern for the first method mentioned usually starts with his **'Current Situation'** Questions like *'Where is the client now, Who is he dealing with, for how long and how satisfied is he'?*

This is where they are **'now'**. These questions are at most times factual and most times available either on their websites or from others around but are used to help start the conversation and build rapport. So we usually recommend that you do not ask many of these.

We then gradually move to the **'Desired Situation'** of where does the customer want to be or should be, with Questions like *'What would they like the ideal service levels/ situation to be or What would they like to see or have from an ideal vendor'*. The answers to these questions will tell us the customer's future plans or where they should be or want to be.

The next set of questions, are pertaining to the '**Barriers'** that are in his way, that are preventing him from reaching the desired situation. This is the key that will enable him open his eyes. Sometimes, just one question here could open up opportunities. Barrier questions most times begin with: *'What is* *preventing you from... "What is stopping you from...What is coming in the way of..."*

Here are some examples of these 3 types of Questions:

Current:

What are your upcoming Projects?

What is the current status of the Project?

How long have you been dealing with this Service Provider?

Desired:

What are your Customer's expectations?

How happy are you with the Service of the existing provider and what would you like it to be?

What are your expectations in having these resolved?

How do you plan to address these issues?

What would you like to happen to ensure a smooth working?

Barriers:

What are the factors coming in the way of you creating/maintaining a good brand Image?

What are the factors stopping you from maintaining a problem free situation?

What are the parameters which are preventing you to achieve.....?

The second method as mentioned earlier is the **C.O.R.K.** Model- **C.O.R.K.** standing for: **C**urrent Circumstances, **O**bstacles, **R**epercussions and **K**ey for Solution.

You could begin with the Current situation on the circumstances or Factual Questions, to help you start building a rapport to move on. Caution again here is not to ask too many of these Questions, since these are factual and it may seem or give the impression that you have not done prior work...So limit it to a few just to help you get started.

The next set of questions are the ones that can help open up on the Obstacles or Problems your customer is currently facing. Most times the customer will not even realize that they are sitting on a problem! Sometimes for years they could be living with this pain or problem without realizing. This is the real pain that his company could be going through. So effective Questions here can help them open up on this pain.

The third set of Questions deal with the Repercussions that these pains or problems could have or cause or lead to if not handled on time or not handled now! This creates the urgency for a change now! This is the subtle fear part that will help the customer make a change or decide to listen further to you.

The fourth set of Questions- the 'Key for Solution' is the step of asking the customer of what they think a good solution might be, which helps in promoting a platform for your solution and gain commitment from them on the usefulness of this proposed solution from you.

These four questions could be around the following key areas depending on your products or services:

- ✓ The Contacts or Decision Makers or Purchasing Process
- ✓ Current Supplier/Pricing
- ✓ Needs (long term/volume)
- ✓ The Organization size
- ✓ Special Delivery Requirements
- ✓ The Decision Making process
- ✓ Problems with Current Supplier (the Pain!)

- ✓ Problems this causes with other departments
- ✓ Other Problems

By being thorough in the preparation of your questions, which is usually done in advance at your preparation stage, you can ensure that nothing is missed and you can move to the next stage of the sales process with all the information you need.

We just covered earlier about the C.O.R.K. Model of Questioning. But I'd like to spend some more time on the 3 most important parts of this model- the **Obstacles,** the **Repercussion,** and **Key for Solution** set of Questions

Obstacle Questions are all about unraveling or probing about concerns, problems, pains, dissatisfactions or difficulties that the buyer is experiencing with the existing situation

Examples of this type of Question would be:

- ✓ *'What makes this operation difficult'?*
- ✓ *'In what areas are you experiencing most difficulties at this time'?*
- ✓ *'What are some of the challenges you are experiencing with your existing supplier now'?*

Repercussion Questions are about the **consequences or effects** of a buyer's problems, difficulties, or dissatisfactions.

Once you have an indication or picture of the type of problem the customer is going through, you would now need to build or draw the customers' attention to the Repercussion or Effect that this problem could have if not acted on time.

Examples of this type of Question would be:

- ✓ *'What effect does that problem have on output'?*
- ✓ *'Could that lead to added costs'?*

- ✓ *'What happens if you do not achieve that goal'?*
- ✓ *'Which other departments are effected'? Or 'Who all are effected with this'?*

As you will see from the discussion that you have with the customer, several Implications can lead from one overriding problem or issue. Linking other possible problems or consequences to a given problem clearly increases its significance and urgency to the Buyer.

The 'Key for Solution' Questions will help you to get your customers to tell you the benefits that your solution can offer by asking them what they think a good solution might be, which can further help promote a platform for your solution and gain commitment from them on the usefulness of this proposed solution from you, when you move to the next step of the Selling Cycle.

Examples of this type of Question would be:

- ✓ *'If you had to do ...., by how much would that save you'?'*
- ✓ *'What would it mean to your customer service if you could have ....fitted or done'?*
- ✓ *'What would it mean to your image and customer service if you could have......?*

Here are some examples of the C.O.R.K. Model of Questions...focusing on the Current Circumstances, Obstacles and the Repercussions. I hope that this will help give you a start in building your own list.

Current Circumstances Questions:

- ✓ Can you describe your current process for [relevant topic]?
- ✓ How long have you been using your current solution?

- ✓ Who is involved in the decision-making process for [relevant topic]?
- ✓ How do you currently measure the effectiveness of [relevant topic]?
- ✓ Are there any specific regulations or standards you need to comply with?
- ✓ What resources are currently allocated to [relevant topic]?
- ✓ How would you rate your satisfaction with your current [relevant topic]?
- ✓ Can you provide an overview of your current [relevant topic] setup?
- ✓ What prompted you to consider a change in your current [relevant topic]?

Obstacles Questions:

- ✓ What issues have you experienced with your current [relevant topic]?
- ✓ How often do these issues occur?
- ✓ How much time do you spend dealing with these issues?
- ✓ *What criteria do your customers judge you on?*
- ✓ *What are the difficulties in working with....?*
- ✓ *Have you ever had a situation where you......*
- ✓ *What were some of the issues you've had to face in the past?*
- ✓ *What are issues you are facing in catering to your customer's expectations?*
- ✓ *How is your current service provider handling your...?*
- ✓ *What is your customer's feedback on the last project?*
- ✓ *What are the improvements you expect with the service that is currently offered?*

- ✓ *While looking for a new vendor what areas are given more priority?*
- ✓ *What areas you feel you are paying excess to your current service provider?*

Repercussions Questions:

- ✓ What impact do these issues have on your operations?
- ✓ How do these issues impact your bottom line?
- ✓ What risks are associated with not addressing these issues?
- ✓ How does this affect your ability to compete in the market?
- ✓ What opportunities are you missing out on due to these issues?
- ✓ How do these issues affect employee morale and retention?
- ✓ Have these issues caused any damage to your reputation?
- ✓ How does this impact your ability to meet customer demands?
- ✓ How do these issues affect your ability to innovate and grow?
- ✓ What long-term consequences do you foresee if these issues persist?
- ✓ How do these issues affect your customers' perception of your brand?
- ✓ *What happens when….?*
- ✓ *How much will that cost your organization?*
- ✓ *How big a problem will that be?*

Key for Solution Questions:

- ✓ *What would it mean competitively, if you could just change or have……?*

- ✓ *How much better would the company image and your customer service be, if you could have...?*
- ✓ *By how much more would you be ahead of the competition if you had to….?*
- ✓ *If you had to do …., by how much would that save you?*
- ✓ How would addressing these issues improve your overall efficiency?
- ✓ What benefits do you expect from implementing a new solution?
- ✓ How would a new solution help you achieve your strategic objectives?
- ✓ How would improved [relevant topic] impact your customer satisfaction?
- ✓ What competitive advantages do you expect from a new solution?
- ✓ How would a new solution support your growth plans?
- ✓ How would a new solution enhance your team's capabilities?
- ✓ What positive outcomes do you envision from addressing these issues?
- ✓ How would a new solution help you stay ahead of market trends?
- ✓ What would success look like for you after implementing a new solution?

Remember: As a Sales Professional, there are 5 important **P's** in Selling. Your job is to first of all uncover the **Problems**, **Pains** and **Predicaments**, and only after which these could give rise to the **Possibilities** for you to **Prescribe**!...Till then, you as the salesperson have no right to do so, and even if you do, this can drastically effect your credibility and

future relationship. It is like a doctor trying to prescribe without diagnosing the case!
Every business owner faces some challenge, and more so during downtimes. To be able to discover the fears, frustration or pain your prospects feel, you have to first build rapport before they can open up to you. Here are some examples to uncover their challenges.
1. What are some of the top challenges in the business?
2. What would an example of this challenge be like?
3. Roughly how much is this challenge costing?
4. What would it mean to you if you could solve this challenge?
5. Keeping the big picture, what are you trying to achieve?
It is also important to find out what frustrations your prospects go through when dealing with you or others. If with others, they could be unique, but if it is with your organization, then hopefully it should open your eyes. Whatever be the answers, these are opportunities for your organization to pitch in. Some examples that they could come up with could be:

- ✓ *Incompetence or too many false claims*
- ✓ *No value in product or service*
- ✓ *Wrong product pushed*
- ✓ *Too expensive*
- ✓ *High risk or no guarantees*
- ✓ *Technology behind others*
- ✓ *Inconvenience*
- ✓ *Poor quality or unreliable*
- ✓ *No return of phone calls*
- ✓ *Lacking documentation*
- ✓ *No support during warranty period*

- ✓ *Unable to reach salesperson who sold the product or service*

After they have revealed all their frustrations, you can probe deeper so your solution discovers a fit. Here are some examples:

- ✓ *How did you resolve it? Tell me more*
- ✓ *What other area of your business was affected because of this challenge?*
- ✓ *Can you paint a picture of an ideal or perfect solution?*
- ✓ *Ultimately, how would you feel resolving this issue?*

Example of Steps you can follow to Uncover the Pain Areas/ Points:

1. Research and Preparation: Before engaging with customers, conduct thorough research on their industry, company, and specific challenges they may be facing. This will enable you to have informed discussions and ask relevant questions. Example: If you are selling cyber-security solutions, research industry trends, recent data breaches, and common security challenges faced by businesses in the customer's sector.
2. Active Listening: Engage in active listening during customer interactions to understand their needs and pain points. Encourage open dialogue and ask probing questions to gain deeper insights into their challenges.

   Example: Ask questions like, *"What are the biggest hurdles you face in your current data management processes?"* or *"What are the obstacles or challenges you experience when it comes to optimizing your production line efficiency?"*

3. Empathy and Understanding: Show empathy towards the customer's challenges and demonstrate a genuine interest in understanding their pain points. This will help build rapport and trust.
   Example: Acknowledge the customer's frustration by saying, *"I understand that managing your network security is a complex task. Can you share some specific concerns you encounter while ensuring data protection?"*
4. Probing for Specifics: Dig deeper to uncover specific pain areas by asking targeted questions. Encourage the customer to provide specific examples or describe scenarios where they face difficulties or inefficiencies.
   Example: Ask questions like, *"Can you describe a recent incident where your current software solution fell short in meeting your data analysis needs?"* or *"What are the specific challenges your team faces when it comes to collaboration and document sharing?"*
5. Follow-Up Questions: Ask follow-up questions to explore the impact of the identified pain points on the customer's business operations, productivity, revenue, or customer satisfaction.
   Example: Follow up on a pain point related to slow response times by asking, *"How does the slow response time affect your customer support team's ability to resolve customer issues promptly?"*
6. Summarize and Validate: Summarize the pain points identified during the conversation and validate your understanding with the

customer. This demonstrates your attentiveness and ensures alignment. Example: Recap the pain points by saying, *"So, if I understand correctly, your current inventory management system lacks real-time visibility, leading to inventory stock-outs and delays in order fulfillment. Is that correct?"*

7. Quantify the Impact: Probe further to determine the magnitude of the pain points and their impact on the customer's business. Quantify the potential benefits of addressing these pain points to highlight the value of your solution. Example: Ask questions like, *"Do you have an estimate of the financial losses incurred due to inventory stock-outs?"* or *"How much time does your team spend on manual data entry tasks, and what are the potential cost savings if those tasks were automated?"*

By following these steps, you will be able to effectively uncover the pain areas or pain points that technical customers face. This understanding enables you to position your products or solutions as tailored remedies to address their challenges, ultimately increasing the likelihood of a successful sale.

Sample Open Questions to help Uncover the Need or Pain Areas of your Customer

1. Can you describe your current technical infrastructure and the challenges you face with it?
2. What specific goals or objectives are you trying to achieve with a technical solution?
3. How does your current technology setup impact your productivity or efficiency?

4. Can you elaborate on any bottlenecks or roadblocks that you frequently encounter in your technical processes?
5. What are the biggest pain points or frustrations you experience when it comes to your technical operations?
6. Are there any specific compliance or security requirements that your organization needs to adhere to?
7. How do you measure the success or effectiveness of your current technical systems?
8. Are there any areas where you believe your competitors have a technological advantage over your organization?
9. Can you identify any missed opportunities or areas for improvement within your current technical setup?
10. What are the key factors you consider when evaluating a new technical solution or vendor?
11. How do you envision your ideal technical infrastructure or solution?
12. What outcomes or results are you looking to achieve by implementing a new solution?
13. Are there any upcoming projects or initiatives where a technical solution would play a critical role?
14. How do you anticipate your technical needs will change in the next 12-24 months?
15. Can you provide examples of any recent technical challenges or incidents that have had a significant impact on your operations?
16. What level of scalability or flexibility do you require from a solution?

17. How do you currently handle data management, storage, and analysis?
18. Are there any specific integration requirements with existing systems or software?
19. Can you describe the decision-making process within your organization when it comes to adopting new technical solutions?
20. How would you define a successful partnership with a technical sales provider?

What should the Sequential Pattern be in this stage?

1. A good way to begin is always start with Open Questions (Using either of the Questioning patterns mentioned above ie; Current, Desired, Barriers or Current Circumstances, Obstacles, Repercussions and Key for Solution)
2. Listen attentively
3. Take Notes
4. Clarify/ Reconfirm with Closed Questions

A Professional Salesperson ideally follows a sequential pattern at this stage, starting with Open Questions to uncover the Pain, Problems and their Repercussions and further follows it with Questions on the Key for Solutions.

While the customer talks, you as a Sales person would need to listen attentively.

'People were designed with two ears and one mouth, and that is the ratio in which to use them!'

How to be a good listener?

One of the greatest skills that you as a Sales Person can develop is the skill of listening. The best salespeople are the ones that do less talking and more of listening and that is why I believe God gave us two ears and one mouth- so we would do more listening than talking!

Here are some keys to be an “active” listener:

- ✓ Suspend judgment, initially- Keep an open mind
- ✓ Focus on the speaker and what he is saying including his body language
- ✓ Never interrupt while the customer speaks
- ✓ Tolerate silence. Silence can initially be uneasy, but if you practice tolerating it, you will find it very beneficial especially when negotiating.
- ✓ Listen for facts and key words
- ✓ Avoid distractions; when on the telephone, don’t carry on side conversations; when face-to-face make eye contact
- ✓ Assess what you’ve heard
- ✓ Take notes of key points
- ✓ Clarify and reconfirm what the customer has told you- never assume!
- ✓ Never use your phone in the customers’ premises! It’s a big disturbance and bad manners

Before you respond, assess the information you heard by asking yourself four questions in your mind:

- ✓ *What has the customer told me?*
- ✓ *What can I do with this information?*
- ✓ *What else do I need to know?*
- ✓ *What questions do I still need to ask?*

To show you’re listening actively:

- ✓ Respond by using terms like, *‘Go on’*, *Uh huh’* and ‘*mmm*’
- ✓ Stay tuned in; Watch for non-verbal cues
- ✓ To show that you have, understood:

- ✓ Use, phrases like *"I see," "I understand"*
- ✓ Paraphrase, *"So you want me to …"*

Taking Notes

A professional sales person will always takes notes of key points and never depend on memory.

By taking notes you are subtly telling the customer:

- ✓ *I care about your business*
- ✓ *I do not want to miss anything*
- ✓ *The competition came by, but was more interested in the order, I am here to help!*
- ✓ *I am a professional*

Clarifying and Reconfirming with Closed Questions

This is the time when closed questions are very useful. To clarify and reconfirm, restate in your own words what the client has said and ask him to verify your understanding. An example would be: *'Mr Customer, Let me just take a minute to summarize, just to ensure that I've got the right information…You were mentioning that you were having a problem with….Am I right Mr. So and So?"* After the other person has confirmed your understanding, you have earned the right to proceed with additional questions to gain more information about the situation.

Why summarize regularly?

- ✓ *It keeps complexities under control*
- ✓ *It tests progress*
- ✓ *It lets you restate what the other party has said*
- ✓ *It can help gain the initiative*
- ✓ *It can keep the discussion on track*
- ✓ *It can prevent misinterpretation, misunderstanding and subsequent bitterness*

In other words, summarizing helps you stay on top. By summarizing, you are making sure you have the right information and that you haven't left out anything.

Understanding How the Client Defines Value

Understanding how a client defines value is crucial in sales, as it allows you to tailor your offering to meet their specific needs and priorities. Here are the steps involved in understanding how a client defines value, along with examples:

1. **Research and Preparation**: Conduct research on the client's industry, market trends, and competitors to understand their business environment. Identify key decision-makers and stakeholders.
   Example: For a software salesperson, researching the client's industry may reveal that their competitors are using a specific software feature to gain a competitive edge.
2. **Engage in Meaningful Conversations**: Have open and honest conversations with the client to understand their challenges, goals, and priorities. Ask probing questions to uncover their definition of value.
   Example: Ask the client about their current challenges with their existing software and how they measure success in this area.
3. **Listen Actively**: Listen attentively to the client's responses and take note of key themes and priorities. Pay attention to not just what they say, but also how they say it and what is left unsaid.
   Example: If the client emphasizes the need for seamless integration with other systems, it indicates that interoperability is a key value driver for them.

4. **Identify Value Drivers**: Identify the key factors that drive value for the client. These could include cost savings, increased efficiency, improved customer satisfaction, or other specific outcomes they are seeking.
   Example: If the client mentions that they are looking to reduce operational costs, cost-effectiveness and efficiency become important value drivers for them.
5. **Align Solutions with Client Value Drivers**: Tailor your solutions to align with the client's value drivers. Highlight how your offering addresses their specific needs and delivers value in areas that are important to them.
   Example: If cost-effectiveness is a key value driver, emphasize how your software can help them reduce costs through efficiency gains.
6. **Quantify Value**: Where possible, quantify the value of your offering in terms that are meaningful to the client. This could include cost savings, revenue increases, or other tangible benefits.
   Example: Calculate the potential cost savings the client could achieve by using your software compared to their current solution.
7. **Present Value Proposition**: Present your value proposition to the client in a clear and compelling manner. Demonstrate how your offering provides value in line with their definition of value.
   Example: Present a case study or success story of a similar client who achieved significant cost savings and efficiency gains by using your software.

8. **Seek Feedback**: Throughout the sales process, seek feedback from the client to ensure that you are aligning with their definition of value. Make adjustments to your approach as needed.
   Example: Ask the client if they believe your solution meets their definition of value and if there are any additional features or benefits they would like to see.
9. **Continuously Improve**: Use feedback from clients and insights from the sales process to continuously improve your understanding of how clients define value and refine your value proposition accordingly.
   Example: Incorporate feedback from clients into future sales pitches to better align with their definition of value.

By following these steps and actively engaging with clients, you can gain a deeper understanding of how they define value and position your offering to meet their specific needs and priorities.

Identifying and Aligning with Client Value

Understanding and aligning with the client's values and priorities are essential for building successful and long-lasting relationships. This process involves identifying the client's pressure points, defining value from their perspective, and aligning your solutions with their needs and expectations.

Identifying Pressure Points

Pressure points are the specific challenges or issues that clients are facing, which create a sense of urgency or importance for them. By identifying these pressure points, sales professionals can tailor their solutions to address these specific needs and demonstrate the value of their offerings.

For example, a client may be experiencing pressure to reduce costs due to budget constraints or increase efficiency to meet tight deadlines. By understanding these pressure points, sales professionals can position their solutions as ways to alleviate these pressures and deliver tangible benefits to the client.

How Does the Client Define Value?

Client value can be defined in various ways, depending on the client's priorities and objectives. For some clients, value may be defined in terms of cost savings or efficiency gains, while for others, it may be about achieving specific outcomes or gaining a competitive advantage.

To align with the client's definition of value, sales professionals must first understand how the client perceives value. This involves asking probing questions to uncover the client's needs, priorities, and objectives. By understanding the client's definition of value, sales professionals can tailor their solutions to meet these specific needs and demonstrate the value of their offerings.

Examples

An example of a company that excels in identifying and aligning with client value is Microsoft. Microsoft offers a range of products and services that are designed to meet the diverse needs of its clients, from small businesses to large enterprises. By understanding the unique challenges and priorities of each client segment, Microsoft is able to tailor its solutions to deliver maximum value to its clients.

Another example is Apple, which has built a strong brand reputation by aligning its products with the values and priorities of its customers. Apple's products are known for their innovative design, ease of use, and seamless integration, all of which align with the values of its target audience.

Action Plan & Strategies

To identify and align with client value, sales professionals can follow these action plans and strategies:

- ✓ Conduct thorough research: Before engaging with a client, conduct research to understand their business, industry, and competitors. This will help you identify their pressure points and define value from their perspective.
- ✓ Ask probing questions: During your interactions with the client, ask probing questions to uncover their specific needs, priorities, and objectives. This will help you align your solutions with their expectations.
- ✓ Tailor your solutions: Based on your research and the client's feedback, tailor your solutions to meet their specific needs and address their

pressure points. Focus on highlighting the value that your offerings can deliver to the client.

- ✓ Provide evidence and testimonials: Use case studies, testimonials, and other forms of evidence to demonstrate the value of your solutions to the client. This will help build credibility and trust with the client.
- ✓ Follow up: After delivering your solutions, follow up with the client to ensure that they are satisfied with the results. This will help you maintain a strong relationship with the client and position yourself as a trusted advisor.

By following these strategies, sales professionals can effectively identify and align with client value, ultimately leading to stronger relationships and increased sales opportunities.

Offering Value and Your Differentiators

Usually the temptation for a Sales Person at this stage, once he's identified the need is to immediately jump into recommending the solution. This can backfire, with a number of objections, as the customer is yet not convinced on the value of your proposition. Therefore, there is one more step, before we actually get to recommend the solution; and that is to build in the mind of the customer the value that your company and the product or service that matches the relevant need identified brings to them. It is similar to what a good waiter would do in a restaurant. Before he takes your order he would literally make your mouth water by talking about the taste of the dishes by building up that appetite in you. So now when he does bring the dish to the table, you are ready to relish it!

To begin, you must ask this question? Are you trying to sell your services or solve problems for your clients? If people you are selling to, see you as wanting to sell them something, then right now, they are scared, short on cash, and not interested in buying anything, and can see what you do as an expense and not a sure way to reduce costs or drive new sales. Find ways therefore to directly deal with people's fears. Your prospects are more afraid than ever to spend money. You need to prove the value of your services with real examples- on how to reduce costs and help them gain a competitive advantage.

So there is a shift in our thinking that must take place. In this economy, you can't just sell by simply telling people about your services. You really have to understand the value of what you sell, how your clients will use your products and services, and how using your products will change their business for the better. Don't sell your company and don't sell your products or services, but instead, focus on the results of using your products or services. Find ways you can show every prospect how you can reduce their current expenses and enable their company to sell more.

So how do you make the most of your competitive advantage? You need to understand your product's value, its position in the market, and, most importantly, its competitive advantage.

- ✓ Are you faster?
- ✓ Better quality?
- ✓ Are you least expensive?
- ✓ Or do you have the best customer service?

The answer to these questions will dictate your sales approach, as you will need to not only lean on your competitive advantage, but you'll need to drill this in and find the prospects who are most likely to be looking for whatever it is your company is uniquely positioned to offer.

Proving value allows you to show the client why your product or service is an effective one and the value it brings to them, before you show the client how you can help them solve a problem/need or realize an opportunity with your recommendation.

Whenever people buy anything, there are two aspects that they are concerned about:

1. What will the relevant product/ services do for my company- How will it help me? What value will we get from this?

2. Who or Which is the company behind this? Their standing? Will they support me when I need them? The Reliability Factor!

Let us look at the Product or Service first:

There are 3 aspects to your products or services. The **Features, Advantages** and **Benefits**

A Feature describes some '*characteristics*' of a product or service. Features are relatively neutral, both in their content and in their effect on the buyer. Features are those aspects of a product, or service that we can see, or describe. It is usually what the manufacturer or producer '*has put into*' the product.

Example: Let us take a simple example that anyone can understand...

- ✓ *This mobile phone has a 'hands-free' facility*

When presenting features it is important to emphasize only those features that the customer said were most important to the customer during the probing phase of the sales process. These relate to the customers' buying criteria.

Now a number of Sales people lose out big time because they rattle 'only' the features of the product or service they are representing. And because of this the customer does not see the perceived value, because sometimes this could just sound technical and go over his head!

We need to translate the relevant feature into an ultimate Benefit. In other words '*what will it do'* for the customer! Again, some sales people make the mistake of mentioning all of the features of the product or service that they could think of during their presentation.

This is not helpful at all, but on the contrary confusing and can actually deter the customer from making a positive buying decision. It can seem that the sales person wasn't listening effectively during the questioning phase of the sales process.

So as a Sales person, it is for you now to translate this relevant Feature or Features that you just spoke of into an Advantage

An Advantage describes how a product, or a product feature, can be used or can help the buyer during the buying process.

Advantages, as you will see are more persuasive than features. ***Salespeople who talk about advantages sell more than salespeople who feature dump.***

Building on the same example:

- ✓ *Because this mobile has a hand-free facility, you can use it safely to answer calls, while driving when the car is in motion*

At this stage, we need to remind ourselves that people buy because they have needs. If you as the seller can relate the product or service specifically to those needs identified in the earlier step, then there is a high probability of making a sale.

Benefits describe how the features and advantages will affect the buyer individually. They relate to the emotional buying behavior. In other words, the key is: ***what will the product or service do*** for them!

The key benefit words and statements are reassurance, confidence and peace of mind.

Asking questions in the earlier stage was to identify needs. Once we have identified the buyers' main buying criteria we can link the appropriate Features to the relevant Advantages and Benefits.

- ✓ Think **FAB!**

Going back now to our earlier example of the mobile phone…

Because our mobile has a hand-free facility you can be confident that if a customer calls you in the car, you can respond to the call quickly and safely and not miss out on vital enquiries or business opportunities.

Every business has 5 main needs and your Benefit must address <u>one</u> or <u>more</u> of these …they are the **5** P's…

- ✓ **Profit**- to make more money, that's why they are in business- savings, cost reductions etc
- ✓ **Protection**- to ensure the security and safety of their business/ lives/ property etc,
- ✓ **Peace**-A good night's sleep with no botheration or worry
- ✓ **Prestige-**Wanting to stand out-Image! (for some!)
- ✓ **Performance-** Improved productivity, more efficiency etc

In the example that we just covered, you will notice that the customer benefits by:

1. Business calls that could come in while he is driving: more revenue!
2. Safety while driving
3. To some- even prestigious using a 'hands-free' and driving

What is one phone call worth to him? If on an average he gets 10 business calls when driving, that could be the amount of business potential he could be missing out if not attended to. So now the customer begins to see value in this feature of the product.

It is like an 'FM Radio Frequency' existing between the Buyer and Seller! **'WII-FM'**. It is like the customer always sending out signals of… **W**hat **I**s **In** **I**t **F**or **M**e?

And until this Question is answered by the sales person, the Customer will never proceed!

What to keep in Mind when working on Solutions…

- ✓ The customer's vision-short term/ long term
- ✓ The customer's key Challenges/ Pains and Requirements

Some examples might include:

- ✓ *Cost reduction;*
- ✓ *Improvement in quality;*
- ✓ *Improvement in end – user satisfaction;*
- ✓ *Regulatory or legislation changes;*
- ✓ *Capacity increase;*
- ✓ *Innovation;*
- ✓ *Reduction of customer's 'churn' (customers' moving away);*
- ✓ *Increase in diversity of offering (adding new products or services);*
- ✓ *Replacement of previous or incumbent supplier*

Examples of Features, Advantages and Benefits and the Value the customer will derive

- ✓ Example: Industrial Automation System
  Feature: Real-time monitoring and control capabilities
  Advantage: Enhanced operational visibility and control over processes
  Benefit and Value: Improved productivity, reduced downtime, and optimized resource allocation. Increased operational efficiency, cost savings, and better decision-making based on real-time data
- ✓ Example: Customer Relationship Management (CRM) Software

Feature: Centralized customer database with contact management
Advantage: Streamlined customer interactions and improved data organization
Benefit and Value: Enhanced customer satisfaction, personalized communication, and efficient sales pipeline management. Stronger customer relationships, increased sales revenue, and improved customer retention

- ✓ Example: Cyber-security Solution
  Feature: Advanced threat detection and prevention mechanisms
  Advantage: Robust protection against cyber threats and data breaches
  Benefit and Value: Mitigated risks, safeguarded sensitive information, and ensured regulatory compliance. Enhanced data security, minimized financial losses, and protected brand reputation
- ✓ Example: Enterprise Resource Planning (ERP) System
  Feature: Integrated modules for finance, inventory, and production management
  Advantage: Centralized data and streamlined processes across departments
  Benefit and Value: Improved operational efficiency, optimized resource allocation, and accurate financial insights. Increased productivity, cost savings, and better decision-making based on real-time data integration
- ✓ Example: High-speed Networking Router
  Feature: Gigabit Ethernet ports for fast data transfer
  Advantage: Reliable and high-performance network connectivity

Benefit and Value: Faster data transfer, minimized latency, and improved network efficiency

- ✓ Example: Advanced Security Camera System
  Feature: High-resolution video capture and night vision capability
  Advantage: Comprehensive surveillance and monitoring
  Benefit and Value: Enhanced security, reduced risks of theft or vandalism, and improved safety measures
- ✓ Example: Energy-efficient HVAC System
  Feature: Smart thermostat with programmable settings
  Advantage: Optimal energy usage and cost savings
  Benefit and Value: Reduced energy bills, increased comfort, and environmentally friendly operation

By converting the features of these products into advantages and benefits, customers can clearly understand the value they will derive from using the products, by helping them see how the features directly address their needs, solve their pain points, and provides tangible benefits that enhance their operations and outcomes.

As mentioned, the other aspect of Proving Value has to do with the company that is backing the relevant product or service. When Proving Value of your Company, it is important to keep in mind the USP's of your company or 'Unique Selling Propositions'

- ✓ *What is it that makes your company stand out from the others?*
- ✓ *What is so special about your company?*

- ✓ *Why should the customer move from his current vendor to deal with your company?*

Your USP's have to be strong enough for it to draw the customer to you! Few pointers are suggested below that can help you think further:

- ✓ *Stability of Company/ Expertise*
- ✓ *Years of Standing*
- ✓ *Special Service Features/ Capabilities*
- ✓ *Terms and Conditions*
- ✓ *Creativity*
- ✓ *Alliances and Partnerships*
- ✓ *Leveraging outside resources and partners network to service our clients*
- ✓ *Awards/ Recognitions*

Here are some key points to keep in mind:

- ✓ You also have to help clients see the risks of doing nothing. While you can't be overly negative or pushy, you have to find effective ways to open their eyes and make people see that by not investing into your products or services right now may be a bigger risk than investing. In other words, the actual money they invest with you will probably not put their business at risk. But on the contrary, not making smart investments will definitely put their business at risk.
- ✓ Look at what can you change in your products, services, processes, systems, and delivery to serve them best now?
- ✓ Get creative with your proposals. Make it irresistible to use your products or services. This can include volume discounts, deals on combinations of services and extended financing terms. Making a few adjustments to

payment options and contract terms can also help to great extents in addressing customers' budgetary concerns.

- ✓ Refocus on delivering value, building trust, not hitting quotas -Instead of obsessing over quota attainment, find ways to deliver more value and support to your existing customer base so they know their investment is worthwhile — and you are there, and will be there throughout their journey.
- ✓ Don't waste time with businesses that can't afford your products or services. If you've called on businesses in good times and failed to buy, they are never going to use your products in bad times either. Be more proactive in reaching out to companies that you want to work with. Figure out which types of companies would be your IDEAL clients, and then get aggressive about winning their business.

Standing out from your Competition!

This is an interesting Exercise you could undertake every time you are making a proposal to a customer.

As we have seen above, people make decisions based on what the product or service will do for them, along with the company backing this.

Keeping the Product/ Service and the company backing it, we can now say that customers would be ideally seeking **Value** on one hand and **Uniqueness** on the other.

So list all features of your offering that you think makes you **Unique** (from the customers' angle or perception) and the perceived **Value** to the Customer (ideally about 10 to 15)

S. No.	Feature	Uniqueness	Value
1.	Example 1	8	9
2.			
3.			
4.			
5.			
6.			
7.			
8.			
9.			
10.			

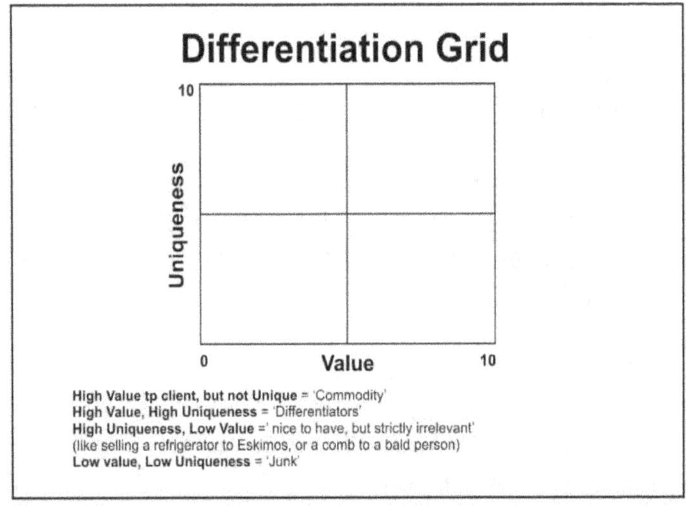

Rate **Uniqueness** and **Value** respectively (on a 0 to 10 scale based on how you feel the customer perceives it)

Remember: What can be relevant for one client can be irrelevant for other clients!

Now plot them on a Quadrant with **Value** on **x axis** and **Uniqueness** on the other **y axis**

Once you've plotted these features on to the 4 quadrants, we now need to see what is of relevance, so we could use only those features that matter to the client, based on the need identified…

When its **High on Value** and **High on Uniqueness**- then these are your **key 'Differentiators'** (The ones appearing in the top right hand corner quadrant)

The features that are in this quadrant are the ones that only you are offering. These are your differentiators. If done really well, then this could indicate that this is what makes you stand out!

High on Value to the client, but **not Unique**, is a **'Commodity'** (the bottom right quadrant)

Any feature appearing in this quadrant is what your competition is also offering- just like you! Nothing great! When you start talking these features, you are on the same battle ground as your competition. The customer now compares you with others.

High Uniqueness and **Low in Value** could be 'nice to have, but strictly irrelevant' to the customer (Top left hand corner) – It does not make sense at all to the customer. The need and the relevant features are a mismatch (like trying to sell a fridge to Eskimos or a comb to a bald person!)

When it is **Low in Value** and **Low in Uniqueness**, just discard these as 'Junk'(Bottom left quadrant)- Don't even look at them or talk of them!

Developing a Value Proposition

A value proposition is a statement that summarizes the unique benefits that a product or service provides to its customers. It is a key component of any successful sales strategy, as it helps to differentiate your offering from competitors and communicate the value that you can deliver to customers. Developing a strong value proposition requires careful planning and consideration, as well as a deep understanding of your target market and their needs.

Develop Plan: Develop Value Proposition

The first step in developing a value proposition is to clearly define the benefits that your product or service offers to customers. This involves identifying the key features and attributes of your offering that set it apart from competitors and provide value to customers. For example, if you are selling a software product, you might highlight features such as ease of use, scalability, and integration with other systems.

Once you have identified the key benefits of your offering, you can begin to develop your value proposition. This should be a concise statement that clearly communicates the unique value that your product or service provides to customers. For example, your value proposition might be *"Our software helps businesses increase productivity and efficiency by streamlining their workflow and automating repetitive tasks."*

Compare to Competitors

It is also important to consider how your value proposition compares to those of your competitors. This involves identifying the key strengths and weaknesses of competing offerings and positioning your own offering in a way that highlights its unique advantages. For example, you might compare your software to a competitor's by highlighting its lower cost, faster implementation time, or better customer support.

Quantify the Value

Another important aspect of developing a value proposition is to quantify the value that your offering provides to customers. This could involve calculating the cost savings, revenue increases, or other tangible benefits that customers can expect to receive by using your product or service. For example, you might quantify the value of your software by estimating the time and cost savings that it can generate for a typical customer.

Value Story

Finally, it is important to develop a compelling value story that reinforces your value proposition and resonates with customers. This involves crafting a narrative that highlights the key benefits of your offering and demonstrates how it can address the specific needs and challenges of your target market. For example, you might tell a story about how a customer used your software to streamline their operations and achieve significant cost savings.

Examples

An example of a company with a strong value proposition is Slack, a business communication platform. Slack's value proposition is "Where work happens." This simple statement communicates the unique benefit of Slack's platform, which is to provide a central hub for team communication and collaboration.

Another example is Dropbox, a file hosting service. Dropbox's value proposition is "Simplify your work with Dropbox." This statement emphasizes the simplicity and ease of use of Dropbox's platform, which is a key selling point for many customers.

Action Plan & Strategies

To develop a strong value proposition, sales professionals can follow these action plans and strategies:

- ✓ Conduct market research: Identify the key needs and pain points of your target market, as well as the strengths and weaknesses of competing offerings. This will help you develop a value proposition that is compelling and relevant to your customers.
- ✓ Focus on benefits, not features: When developing your value proposition, focus on the benefits that your offering provides to customers, rather than just its features. This will help you communicate the value of your offering more effectively.
- ✓ Test and refine your value proposition: Once you have developed your value proposition, test it with customers to see how they respond. Use their feedback to refine and improve your value proposition over time.
- ✓ Use storytelling: Incorporate storytelling into your value proposition to make it more engaging and memorable. Use real-life examples and case studies to illustrate the value that your offering provides to customers.

By following these strategies, sales professionals can develop a strong value proposition that differentiates their offering from competitors and resonates with customers, ultimately leading to increased sales and customer loyalty.

Demonstrating Value

Demonstrating the value of your product or service is essential in sales. It involves showcasing how your offering meets the needs and solves the problems of your potential customers. This chapter explores strategies to effectively demonstrate value, including preparing a business proposal, positioning your solution, and presenting to decision-makers.

Preparing a Business Proposal: A well-crafted business proposal is a key tool for demonstrating value. It should clearly outline the customer's needs, how your product or service addresses those needs, and the expected outcomes. Include case studies, testimonials, and ROI projections to strengthen your proposal.

Example: A software company preparing a proposal for a new CRM system includes case studies from previous clients showing increased sales and customer satisfaction after implementing their software.

Positioning Your Solution: Positioning is about how you differentiate your product or service from competitors in the mind of the customer. Highlight your unique value proposition and key benefits that set you apart.

Example: A marketing agency positions itself as a specialist in social media advertising, showcasing its expertise and success stories in this area.

Presenting to Decision-Makers: When presenting your proposal, focus on the benefits and outcomes rather than just features. Tailor your presentation to the needs and priorities of the decision-makers, and be prepared to address any objections or concerns they may have.

Example: A salesperson presenting a new IT solution to a company's CTO emphasizes how the solution will streamline operations and reduce costs, aligning with the CTO's goals.

Action Plan:

- ✓ Research and Preparation: Thoroughly research the customer's needs, challenges, and goals before preparing your proposal.
- ✓ Customization: Tailor your proposal and presentation to each customer, highlighting how your solution specifically addresses their unique needs.
- ✓ Engagement: Engage with decision-makers throughout the process to understand their priorities and concerns, and adjust your approach accordingly.
- ✓ Follow-up: After the presentation, follow up with additional information or answers to any questions that arose during the meeting.
- ✓ Feedback and Iteration: Solicit feedback from customers on your proposals and presentations to continuously improve your approach.

By effectively demonstrating the value of your offering through well-prepared proposals, strategic positioning, and targeted presentations, you can increase your chances of success in sales and build stronger relationships with your customers.

Personalizing the Presentation

One of the most effective ways to demonstrate value to a potential customer is by personalizing your presentation to their specific needs and preferences. This chapter explores strategies for making your presentation personal and aligning it with the client's perspective.

Making Your Presentation Personal: To make your presentation personal, start by researching the client's business, industry, and challenges. Tailor your presentation to address their specific needs and show how your solution can help them achieve their goals.

Example: A marketing consultant preparing a presentation for a potential client in the healthcare industry researches the client's market position, competition, and target audience to tailor the presentation to their specific challenges and opportunities.

Presentation of Data: Value Drivers: When presenting data, focus on value drivers that are important to the client. These may include alternative solutions, product quality, customization options, responsiveness, flexibility, reliability, technical competence, brand image, trustworthiness, pricing, and the time, effort, and energy saved by using your solution.

Example: A software salesperson presenting a new project management tool emphasizes how the software's customization options, reliability, and technical competence can save the client time and improve project outcomes.

Action Plan:

- ✓ Research and Preparation: Conduct thorough research on the client and their industry to understand their needs and challenges.
- ✓ Tailoring the Presentation: Customize your presentation to address the client's specific needs, focusing on the value drivers that are most relevant to them.
- ✓ Engagement and Interaction: Engage with the client during the presentation, asking questions to understand their perspective and concerns.
- ✓ Demonstrating Value: Use examples, case studies, and testimonials to demonstrate how your solution has provided value to similar clients.
- ✓ Follow-up: After the presentation, follow up with the client to address any remaining questions or concerns and to further personalize your proposal based on their feedback.

By personalizing your presentation and aligning it with the client's perspective, you can demonstrate the value of your solution in a way that resonates with the client and increases your chances of success.

Creating Value-added Proposals

A well-crafted proposal is essential for effectively communicating the value of your offering to customers. A value-added proposal goes beyond simply outlining features and pricing; it demonstrates how your product or service addresses the customer's specific needs and adds value to their business. Here's a detailed exploration of creating value-added proposals, including examples and action plans:

1. **Understand Customer Needs**: Before creating a proposal, thoroughly understand the customer's needs, challenges, and objectives. Tailor your proposal to address these specific requirements.
   Example: A software company researching a potential client's business processes discovers inefficiencies that their software can address. Their proposal focuses on how the software improves efficiency and reduces costs.
2. **Highlight Unique Value Proposition**: Clearly articulate the unique value proposition of your offering. Explain how it stands out from competitors and why it is the best solution for the customer.
   Example: A marketing agency highlights its expertise in social media advertising and offers case studies demonstrating successful campaigns for similar clients.
3. **Outline Key Benefits**: Detail the key benefits of your offering and how they directly impact the customer's business. Use specific

examples and metrics to illustrate these benefits.
Example: A construction company outlines how its building materials are more durable and cost-effective, leading to long-term savings for the customer.

4. **Customize Solutions**: Tailor your proposal to meet the specific needs of the customer. Offer customized solutions that address their unique challenges and goals.
Example: A consulting firm offers a range of service packages, allowing the customer to choose the one that best fits their budget and needs.
5. **Provide Evidence and Testimonials**: Include case studies, testimonials, and references from satisfied customers to validate the effectiveness of your offering.
Example: A software company includes testimonials from current clients who have seen significant improvements in their operations after implementing the software.
6. **Demonstrate ROI**: Clearly outline the return on investment (ROI) that the customer can expect from your offering. Show how the benefits outweigh the costs.
Example: A financial advisor demonstrates how their investment strategies can lead to higher returns compared to traditional savings methods.
7. **Address Potential Concerns**: Anticipate and address any potential concerns or objections the customer may have. Provide solutions or explanations to alleviate these concerns.

Example: A security company addresses concerns about data privacy by outlining its robust encryption methods and compliance with industry standards.

Action Plan:

- ✓ Proposal Template: Develop a standardized proposal template that includes sections for outlining customer needs, highlighting key benefits, and providing evidence of success.
- ✓ Training and Development: Provide training to sales teams on how to create value-added proposals, including how to tailor proposals to meet customer needs and effectively communicate value.
- ✓ Feedback and Review: Solicit feedback from customers on your proposals to identify areas for improvement. Review and refine your proposal templates based on this feedback.
- ✓ Continuous Improvement: Continuously update your proposal templates and strategies based on customer feedback, industry trends, and competitor offerings.
- ✓ Collaboration with Marketing: Work closely with your marketing team to ensure that your proposals align with your brand messaging and marketing efforts.

By following these tips and action plans, you can create value-added proposals that clearly communicate the benefits of your offering and persuade customers to choose your product or service.

A Proposal Template

Here's a detailed standardized proposal template that covers all the aspects you mentioned:

[Your Company Name]
[Proposal Date]
Proposal for [Customer Name]

1. **Executive Summary** Provide a brief overview of the proposal, including the customer's needs, key benefits of your offering, and a summary of the proposed solution.
2. **Customer Needs** Outline the specific needs and challenges of the customer that your proposal aims to address. Provide details based on your discussions and research.
3. **Proposed Solution** Detail your proposed solution, explaining how it meets the customer's needs and solves their challenges. Include any customization or special features tailored to the customer's requirements.
4. **Key Benefits** Highlight the key benefits of your offering, focusing on how it adds value to the customer's business. Use specific examples and metrics to illustrate these benefits.
5. **Addressing Potential Concerns** Anticipate and address potential concerns or objections the customer may have. Provide solutions or explanations to alleviate these concerns.
6. **Return on Investment (ROI)** Demonstrate the expected return on investment for the customer. Show how the benefits of your solution outweigh the costs and provide a clear timeline for achieving ROI.

7. **Evidence of Success** Include case studies, testimonials, and references from satisfied customers to validate the effectiveness of your offering. Provide real-world examples of how your solution has delivered results for similar clients.

8. **Implementation Plan** Outline the steps involved in implementing your solution, including timelines, resources required, and key milestones. Provide a clear roadmap for the customer to understand the process.

9. **Pricing and Terms** Provide a detailed breakdown of pricing for your offering, including any discounts or special offers. Outline the terms and conditions of the proposal, including payment terms and warranties.

10. **Next Steps** Outline the next steps in the process, including how the customer can proceed with the proposal, timelines for decision-making, and any additional information or resources they may need.

11. **Contact Information** Provide your contact information for any questions or further discussions regarding the proposal.

12. **Appendix** Include any additional supporting documents, such as product specifications, team bios, or additional case studies, to further support your proposal.

Sample Template

This template provides a comprehensive framework for creating a detailed proposal that addresses customer needs, highlights key benefits, addresses potential concerns, demonstrates ROI, and provides evidence of success. Adjust the template as needed to fit your specific proposal requirements and customer needs.

Acme Solutions
Date: March 1, 2024
Proposal for XYZ Corporation

1. Executive Summary

Acme Solutions is pleased to present this proposal to XYZ Corporation to address your need for a comprehensive customer relationship management (CRM) solution. Our proposal outlines a customized CRM system that will streamline your sales process, improve customer interactions, and increase overall efficiency.

2. Customer Needs

XYZ Corporation is seeking a CRM solution to manage customer interactions, track sales leads, and improve customer satisfaction. The current system lacks integration and scalability, leading to inefficiencies and missed opportunities.

3. Proposed Solution

Acme Solutions proposes a customized CRM system tailored to XYZ Corporation's specific needs. The system will include modules for sales automation, marketing automation, customer service, and analytics, providing a comprehensive solution to manage customer interactions across the organization.

4. Key Benefits

- ✓ Improved Sales Efficiency: Streamlined sales processes will help sales teams manage leads more effectively and close deals faster.
- ✓ Enhanced Customer Insights: Advanced analytics will provide valuable insights into customer behavior, enabling targeted marketing campaigns and personalized customer interactions.
- ✓ Scalability: The CRM system can scale with your business, accommodating future growth and expansion.

5. Addressing Potential Concerns

We understand that implementing a new CRM system can be disruptive. Our implementation plan includes comprehensive training for your staff to ensure a smooth transition and minimal downtime.

6. Return on Investment (ROI)

Based on our projections, the ROI for implementing the CRM system is expected to be realized within 12 months. The system will lead to increased sales revenue, improved customer retention, and operational cost savings.

7. Evidence of Success

Acme Solutions has successfully implemented CRM solutions for similar clients in the past, resulting in increased sales productivity and improved customer satisfaction. Testimonials from these clients are available upon request.

8. Implementation Plan

- ✓ Phase 1: Requirement Gathering and System Design (2 weeks)
- ✓ Phase 2: System Development and Configuration (4 weeks)
- ✓ Phase 3: User Training and Testing (2 weeks)

- ✓ Phase 4: Go-live and Support (Ongoing)

9. Pricing and Terms

Total cost for the CRM system implementation is $50,000, with payment terms of 50% upfront and 50% upon completion. The proposal is valid for 30 days from the date of this proposal.

10. Next Steps

We invite XYZ Corporation to review this proposal and schedule a meeting to discuss any questions or further details. Upon acceptance, we will proceed with the implementation plan outlined above.

11. Contact Information

For any inquiries or to discuss this proposal further, please contact:

Jonathan Peters
Sales Manager, Acme Solutions
Email: jonathan.peters@acmesolutions.com
Phone: 123-456-7890

12. Appendix

Case studies of successful CRM implementations
Product specifications and features
Team bios of our CRM implementation specialists

This example illustrates how the template can be used to create a detailed and comprehensive proposal for a CRM solution. Adjustments can be made to fit the specific needs and requirements of the customer and the proposal.

Removing Doubts, Concerns and Objections

Overcoming hesitancy, concerns and objections is a fundamental part of sales. During the Sales Process, even the best salespeople can encounter objections that are difficult to handle. An objection is a concern or question raised by the client that delays or prevents you from proceeding to the next step. By using the right techniques, however, you can handle these objections without losing your focus.

Whenever I come to this part I am always reminded of why farmers place a 'scare- crow' in the middle of a paddy or rice field. The answer is obvious- to scare away the birds. But a clever bird knows that behind this so called 'scare-crow' are juicy grains- or his food!

So also, I believe, that a Champion sales person knows that behind every objection there is a genuine need to buy! The objection in question must however be handled or cleared before progress is made.

Why do you think Customers raise objections?

During the sales process customers will raise objections for many reasons. At some stage, customers could:

- ✓ *Misunderstand something you have said.*
- ✓ *Feel pressurized.*
- ✓ *Are not convinced about your claims.*
- ✓ *Haven't yet made up their mind.*
- ✓ *Have to go back and justify their buying decision to others.*

One of the most common times objections are raised is just <u>before</u> the decision to purchase. In this case the customer is often looking for reassurance that the decision to buy is the right one.

We must understand however, that objections form a natural part of the buying process. Just before making a buying decision the buyer worries about making a mistake. And we all do this every day, even for the smallest purchase, so why get worked up when the customer does so?

So if an objection is raised at this stage, it means that the buyer has an unanswered question or concern that the salesperson has to deal with and it could most times be a positive rather than a negative situation when a customer raises an objection

Mostly, there are **two types** of objections that you will encounter:

Doubt

Indifference

Doubt, sometimes is referred to as distrust, and is expressed when the client doesn't believe something you have said.

Indifference on the other hand is expressed when the client feels that what you have said is not important to him – the client may simply feel that it is not appropriate to his situation.

Both type of objections occur for specific reasons. To overcome an objection, you need to recognize why it occurred and then deal with it, immediately.

Clarifying Objections

Clarify what the objection is (express empathy if appropriate)

Then respond accordingly:

To remove doubt:

a. Refer to a similar situation and/or

b. Offer evidence or proof that what you have said is true

To handle indifference:

a. If based on a misunderstanding or lack of information, explain your point more thoroughly and or

b. Outweigh the indifference with the benefits of your suggested approach

Now we need to deal with the objection: Once you fully understand the nature of the objection then it can be answered in different ways depending on whether it is

- ✓ *A misunderstanding by the customer*
- ✓ *Belief over claims you are making*
- ✓ *A product disadvantage.*

You will now need to verify that the objection is removed or cleared from the mind of the customer and to ensure it does not come up later.

Your next step would be to Advance the sale.

The key to objection handling is to react less quickly when an objection is raised and find out more about the problem. Clarify exactly what the problem is then try to overcome the objection.

Finally, if you have dealt with the objection successfully and it is the right time, close the sale, or move on to the next stage of the sales process.

As an experienced Sales Professional, if you made a list of all the objections you have come across, you will notice that most objections or customer concerns can broadly be classified under **4 key heads**, as you will see in the illustration.

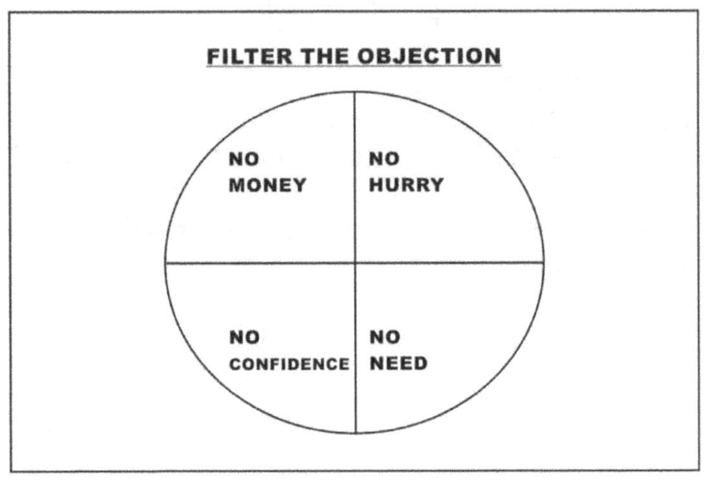

Now try to classify under which quadrant each of your objections fall in under:

For example; if a customer says: *'Your rates are too high'* or *'You guys are very costly'*

Obviously this would feature under the quadrant '**NO MONEY'**

Another example for 'NO MONEY': *'I need a discount!'*

'I don't want to deal with your company again. I had a bad experience last year'!

Or *'Never heard of your company…not too sure about them'!*

Examples like the two above will fall in under the '**NO CONFIDENCE'** Quadrant.

An example of what would come under the quadrant of '**NO HURRY'** would be something like this: *'I am fairly happy with what we have now. We could possibly look at this later only'*

Or *'I don't need any changes right now'* or *'We have enough of this for now'*

The last quadrant '**NO NEED'** is a little tricky and could be something like this: We are n*ot interested'* or *'Please don't see me again'* or *'I don't need you guys'*

Now once you have classified all your objections under the four respective quadrants, let us see what each means and how to go about handling them.

NO MONEY

Do you think the Customer really does not have that additional money?

What he is actually conveying to you by raising that concern that falls in this quadrant is that he does not really see value in your proposition. And most times it will be that the sales person has been rattling off features of his product or service, without really proving value of how the customer will benefit or what it would do for him.

TIP: Keep 'FAB' in mind. Prove value by translating the relevant features to benefits. What is in it for the customer? What will it do for him- translate into tangible benefits that he can see, that far outweighs what he would be investing in.

NO CONFIDENCE

There could be 2 scenarios here:

1. A past customer who has had bad experience and now no more wants to deal with you
2. A new customer who has never heard of you and doubts your company's capability

If it is a past customer, how would we go about building his confidence again in your company and service?

TIP: Show them testimonials of satisfied customers in the same business as theirs, site visits to such customers, case stories of how you resolved similar cases and the outcome, have them connect on phone right away with customers who will talk well of you etc. You could also build on the USP's of your company, particularly relevant to his company and need

If it is a new customer, who has never heard of your company and doubts its capability, then how would we go about instilling and building his confidence in your company and service?

TIP: This is where the USP's prepared under the step Proving Value will help. You could highlight the USP's of your company particularly relevant to his company and need. Show them testimonials of satisfied customers in the same business as theirs, site visits to such customers etc. Particularly of interest would be your Credibility, Standing in the Market, your After-Sales-Support and Financial Status.

NO HURRY

How do we get the customer to take or commit on a decision now?

TIP: Look at what incentives you have now that the customer could benefit by. What if your company does not have the required material when he requires? With the costs of raw materials, labour etc going up, what is the guarantee that he would get your product/ services at this same rate?

NO NEED

Any objection falling in this quadrant is probably one of the most difficult. There are 2 possibilities:

1. There is genuinely no need- He may not be a likely customer
2. He has a need but has not disclosed

If it is the second scenario, then we will need to go back to step 3 of the Selling Skills plan which is Need Uncovering or Probing to uncover further. If the

customer is still unwilling to reveal, then in most times it could be something personal about you as an individual that he is put off with.
TIP: Allow a few days for him to cool down, and then have someone senior from your organization visit them to build up again

Handling the PRICE Objection

Price is probably one of the most common objections we hear in sales. Customers will say *'you are too expensive'*, but before we react, we need to think about what it might mean when they say so.
Sadly, most sales people respond immediately with a *'No Sir....'* rather than trying to understand what was in the customers mind when he said this!

You need to put yourself in the Clients Shoes!

Perceptions Differ! We need to specifically understand...

How short is short!
How firm is firm!
How slim is slim!

As seen from these 2 illustrations, perceptions of individuals differ. So all the more it makes sense to clarify the customers understanding of *'prices are high'* or *'too expensive'* before we hastily jump into handling the same

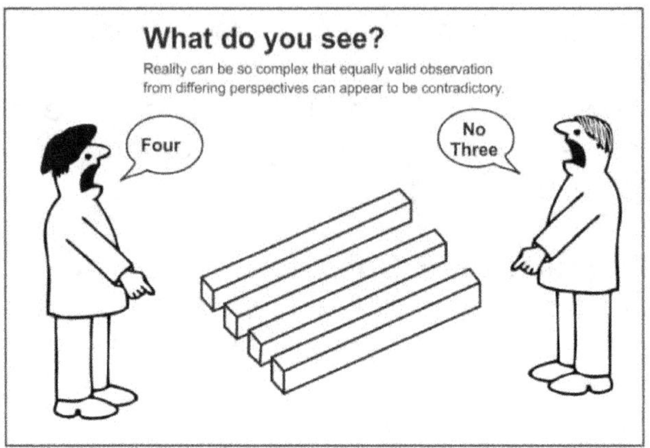

Too expensive could mean several of these and more:

- ✓ *I've had another quote*
- ✓ *I'm checking you out*
- ✓ *I'm negotiating with you*
- ✓ *I have to go back and convince others*
- ✓ *It's more than I expected*
- ✓ *It's more than I have in my budget*
- ✓ *I don't want to buy from you*

This is why it is so important to clarify this objection before we attempt to handle it. We need to find out the real reasons behind the objection. Often we react too quickly and give what we feel is the right answer, but in fact we could be totally wrong.

The customer may have had another quote and may have constituents to satisfy. They may be looking for help etc. Interrupting or not clarifying but giving an inappropriate answer will not help the customer achieve their buying objectives.

Steps to handling an Objection

One of the best ways to answer any sales objection is to:

1. Listen to the objection: Resist the temptation of interrupting the customer. You may have heard the objection a hundred times but not from this particular customer. It may also be that the customer has more than one objection, or that this particular objection is slightly different than the ones you usually hear.
2. Prevent further objections arising: Actually one great way to ensure that this objection never surfaces again or another one does not come up again after you've handled the first one is to ask a question that could go something like this: *'Mr Customer, before I go into answering this concern for you...let me clarify...Is this the only concern that is preventing you from moving forward?"*

In most case the customer will say *'Oh, Yes'*. Now what you've actually done is to indirectly prevent him from coming up with any further excuses in the future!

3. Filter the Objection: See which of the 4 quadrants of NO MONEY, NO HURRY, NO CONFIDENCE, NO NEED (covered above) it falls into
4. If Price, clarify the objection: To clarify the objection you could say something like: *"When you say we are expensive, could you be a little more specific?"*

Listen to what the customer says. He would then clarify why he feels you are expensive. Based on his answer you could take forward. If he is comparing you with the competition, then use your differentiation grid (covered earlier) to stand out.

Key Technical Objections usually faced by Sales Professional

When dealing with technical customers, sales professionals may usually encounter various objections. Here are some key objections you may face along with strategies, steps, and examples to handle each objection effectively:

1. Cost/Price Objection:

- ✓ Strategy: Highlight the value and ROI of your solution.
- ✓ Steps: a. Understand the customer's budget limitations and cost expectations. b. Clearly articulate the long-term benefits and cost savings your solution provides. c. Compare the total cost of ownership and return on investment of your solution against alternative options. d. Offer flexible pricing options, such as financing or phased implementation, to alleviate cost concerns.
- ✓ Example: If a customer raises cost objections, you can demonstrate how your software solution can streamline their processes, reduce operational expenses by 30%, and deliver a payback period of less than a year. Additionally, you can offer a cost-benefit analysis showcasing the financial gains they can achieve by implementing your solution.

2. Technical Compatibility Objection:

- ✓ Strategy: Provide technical expertise and address compatibility concerns.
- ✓ Steps: a. Listen actively to the customer's specific compatibility concerns. b. Offer detailed technical explanations and demonstrations to show how your solution integrates with their existing infrastructure. c.

Provide case studies or testimonials from customers with similar technical environments who have successfully implemented your solution. d. Offer pilot programs or proof-of-concept trials to demonstrate compatibility.

- ✓ Example: If a customer questions the compatibility of your hardware with their existing systems, you can offer a pilot program where they can test the equipment in their environment to ensure seamless integration. Provide detailed documentation and technical specifications to address their concerns and reassure them of the compatibility of your solution.

3. Implementation/Integration Objection:

- ✓ Strategy: Provide a clear implementation plan and support.
- ✓ Steps: a. Understand the customer's implementation challenges and requirements. b. Present a detailed implementation plan outlining the steps, timelines, and resources needed. c. Offer on-site or remote support during the implementation process. d. Provide customer success stories that highlight successful implementations and address potential integration issues.
- ✓ Example: If a customer raises concerns about the complexity of integrating your software into their existing systems, you can offer dedicated implementation support from your technical team. Provide a timeline with specific milestones, conduct training sessions, and offer ongoing assistance to ensure a smooth integration process.

4. Competitor Comparison Objection:

- ✓ Strategy: Highlight your unique selling points and differentiation.
- ✓ Steps: a. Understand the customer's concerns about competitors and their offerings. b. Clearly articulate the unique features and benefits of your solution. c. Emphasize your company's track record, reputation, and customer satisfaction. d. Offer a detailed comparison highlighting the advantages of your solution over competitors.
- ✓ Example: When a customer mentions a competitor, focus on what sets your solution apart. Highlight specific features, performance metrics, or industry recognitions that differentiate your product. Share customer testimonials or case studies that showcase how your solution outperforms the competition in terms of reliability, scalability, or customer support.

5. Risk or Security Objection:

- ✓ Strategy: Address concerns regarding data security or risk mitigation.
- ✓ Steps: a. Understand the customer's specific security or risk-related concerns. b. Provide detailed information about your data security protocols, compliance certifications, and encryption measures. c. Share success stories or case studies of customers in similar industries who have successfully implemented your solution with a focus on risk mitigation. d. Offer risk-free trial periods or satisfaction guarantees to alleviate concerns.
- ✓ Example: If a customer expresses concerns about data security, you can highlight your company's adherence to industry-standard

security protocols, such as ISO certifications or compliance with data protection regulations. Provide documentation that outlines the robust security measures in place to protect customer data and offer a trial period with data encryption to showcase your commitment to data security.

By anticipating and effectively addressing these objections, sales professionals can build trust, overcome customer hesitations, and move closer to closing deals successfully. Remember to listen actively, tailor your responses to the customer's specific concerns, and provide evidence-based solutions to build confidence in your offerings.

Negotiation and Closing Successfully

Negotiation is a critical skill for sales professionals, allowing them to secure deals that benefit both parties involved. The goal of negotiation should be to achieve a win-win outcome where both the sales professional and the customer feel satisfied with the agreement. Here's a detailed exploration of negotiation techniques, including examples and action plans:

1. **Preparation**: Before entering into negotiations, sales professionals should thoroughly prepare by researching the customer's needs, understanding their budget constraints, and identifying areas of flexibility.
   Example: A sales professional preparing to negotiate a contract with a customer researches the customer's industry trends and competitors to understand their position and needs better.
2. **Active Listening**: During negotiations, it's essential to listen actively to the customer's concerns, objectives, and priorities. This helps identify areas where compromises can be made to reach a mutually beneficial agreement.
   Example: A sales professional listens to a customer's feedback on pricing and product features, acknowledging their concerns and seeking ways to address them.
3. **Focus on Value**: Instead of solely focusing on price, emphasize the value that your product or service provides. Help the customer

understand how your offering meets their specific needs and adds value to their business.
Example: In a negotiation, a sales professional highlights the cost savings and efficiency gains that a customer can achieve by using their software solution.

4. **Seek Win-Win Solutions**: Look for creative solutions that meet the needs of both parties. This might involve offering flexible payment terms, bundling products or services, or providing additional value-added services.
   Example: In a negotiation, a sales professional offers a discounted rate for a customer who commits to a long-term contract, benefiting both parties.
5. **Maintain a Positive Relationship**: Building rapport and maintaining a positive relationship with the customer throughout the negotiation process is crucial. This helps create a collaborative atmosphere where both parties can work together to find solutions.
   Example: A sales professional maintains open and honest communication with a customer, addressing any concerns or issues promptly to prevent misunderstandings.

Closing Successfully

Obtaining Customer Commitment: Once you have addressed the client's objections and negotiated, it's time to ask for their commitment. Clearly outline the next steps and what is required from both parties to move forward with the deal.

Example: After addressing all of the client's concerns, you can say, "Based on our discussion today, it seems like our solution meets your needs. Are you ready to move forward with the implementation?"

Discussing Terms and Conditions: Discussing terms and conditions is an important part of closing the deal. Be transparent about pricing, delivery timelines, and any other relevant details to ensure both parties are in agreement.

Example: Present the client with a clear and detailed proposal that outlines the terms and conditions of the deal, including pricing, payment terms, and delivery schedules.

Defining Project KPIs and Plans: Before finalizing the deal, it's important to define key performance indicators (KPIs) and project plans to ensure both parties are aligned on expectations and outcomes.

Example: Work with the client to define specific KPIs for the project, such as sales targets or customer satisfaction metrics, and develop a detailed project plan that outlines the steps and timelines for implementation.

Action Plan:

- ✓ Value Proposition: Clearly articulate the value of your solution in addressing the client's needs and concerns.
- ✓ Provide Evidence: Use examples, case studies, and testimonials to support your responses to objections.
- ✓ Ask for Commitment: Once objections have been addressed, ask the client for their commitment to move forward.
- ✓ Discuss Terms and Conditions: Be transparent about pricing, delivery timelines, and other relevant details.

- ✓ Define Project KPIs and Plans: Work with the client to define KPIs and develop a project plan that aligns with their goals and expectations.

By effectively handling objections, negotiating and closing the deal, you can build stronger relationships with clients and increase your sales success.

Up-selling and Cross-selling

Up-selling and cross-selling are valuable strategies for increasing revenue and providing additional value to customers.
Up-selling involves offering customers a more expensive or upgraded version of a product or service they are already considering, while cross-selling involves offering complementary products or services that add value to the customer's purchase.

Here's a detailed exploration of up-selling and cross-selling strategies, including examples and action plans:

1. **Identifying Opportunities**: To successfully up-sell or cross-sell, sales professionals must first identify opportunities within a customer's business where additional products or services could provide value.
   Example: A sales professional selling a customer a new software system identifies an opportunity to up-sell by offering an upgraded version with additional features that better meet the customer's needs.
2. **Understanding Customer Needs**: Effective up-selling and cross-selling require a deep understanding of the customer's needs and objectives. Sales professionals should listen actively to the customer and identify areas where additional products or services could address their challenges.
   Example: A sales professional offering a customer a new printer also suggests purchasing additional ink cartridges and paper

to ensure they have everything they need to use the printer effectively.

3. **Presenting Relevant Solutions**: When up-selling or cross-selling, it's essential to present solutions that are relevant to the customer's needs and provide clear benefits.
   Example: A sales professional offering a customer a new website design also suggests adding a monthly maintenance package to ensure the website remains secure and up-to-date.
4. **Highlighting Value**: Emphasize the value that additional products or services will bring to the customer. Explain how these offerings will enhance their experience or help them achieve their goals.
   Example: A sales professional offering a customer a new CRM system highlights how the system's advanced reporting features will help them track and analyze customer data more effectively.
5. **Timing and Relevance**: Up-selling and cross-selling should be done at the right time and in a way that is relevant to the customer's current purchase or situation.
   Example: A sales professional offering a customer a new smart-phone also suggests purchasing a protective case and screen protector to keep the phone safe.

Action Plan:

- ✓ Customer Needs Analysis: Conduct a thorough analysis of customer needs and objectives to identify up-selling and cross-selling opportunities.

- ✓ Training and Development: Provide training to sales teams on up-selling and cross-selling techniques, including how to identify opportunities and present relevant solutions.
- ✓ Sales Collateral: Develop sales collateral that highlights the benefits of up-selling and cross-selling offerings, making it easier for sales professionals to present these options to customers.
- ✓ Incentives and Rewards: Offer incentives or rewards to sales professionals for successful up-sells and cross-sells, encouraging them to actively seek out these opportunities.
- ✓ Monitoring and Evaluation: Monitor up-selling and cross-selling efforts to track success rates and identify areas for improvement. Use this data to refine strategies and approaches.

Steps for Up-selling and Cross-selling from Different Industries

Upselling Steps:

1. Understand Customer Needs: Identify the customer's primary need or purchase and understand how a higher-tier product or service could better fulfill that need.
2. Recommend Relevant Upgrades: Suggest upgrades that provide added value or additional features that align with the customer's needs.
3. Highlight Benefits: Clearly explain the benefits of the upgrade, focusing on how it enhances the customer experience or solves additional problems.
4. Overcome Objections: Address any concerns the customer may have about the upgrade,

such as price or compatibility, with compelling arguments.

5. Close the Sale: Encourage the customer to upgrade by offering incentives or discounts and making the process seamless.

Upselling Examples:

- ✓ Tech Industry: A customer buying a laptop is offered a higher-end model with more storage and processing power.
- ✓ Hospitality Industry: A guest booking a standard room is offered an upgrade to a suite with additional amenities.
- ✓ Retail Industry: A shopper buying a smartphone is offered a more advanced model with better camera quality and features.
- ✓ Automotive Industry: A car buyer is offered an upgrade to a vehicle with more advanced safety features and technology.
- ✓ Financial Services Industry: A client opening a basic savings account is offered an account with higher interest rates and additional benefits.

Cross-selling Steps:

1. Identify Related Products: Determine which products or services complement the customer's initial purchase and add value to their overall experience.
2. Recommend Relevant Add-ons: Suggest add-on products or services that enhance the customer's primary purchase and provide additional benefits.
3. Explain the Value: Clearly communicate how the add-on products or services enhance the

customer's experience or solve additional problems.

4. Bundle Products Together: Offer bundled packages that include the customer's primary purchase along with related products or services at a discounted rate.
5. Make it Easy to Purchase: Provide a seamless purchasing process for the add-on products or services, making it convenient for the customer to buy.

Cross-selling Examples:

- ✓ E-commerce Industry: A customer buying a camera is offered a bundle that includes a memory card, camera bag, and tripod.
- ✓ Fitness Industry: A gym member signing up for a membership is offered personal training sessions and nutritional counseling.
- ✓ Telecommunications Industry: A customer purchasing a phone plan is offered a bundle that includes a phone case, screen protector, and charger.
- ✓ Food Industry: A customer ordering a burger is offered a combo meal that includes fries and a drink.
- ✓ Insurance Industry: A policyholder purchasing car insurance is offered a bundle that includes home insurance at a discounted rate.

These examples demonstrate how upselling and cross-selling can be applied across various industries to increase revenue and provide added value to customers.

Arranging Product Demos

Importance and Benefits of Product Demos in Technical Sales

Product demos play a crucial role in technical sales by providing a hands-on experience for customers and showcasing the features, functionality, and value of a product or solution. Here are some of the key importance and benefits of product demos in technical sales:

- ✓ Effective Communication: Product demos allow sales professionals to communicate complex technical information in a clear and understandable manner. They provide a visual and interactive way to demonstrate the product's capabilities and benefits, making it easier for customers to grasp the value proposition.
- ✓ Enhanced Understanding: A product demo helps customers gain a deeper understanding of how the product works and how it can address their specific needs or pain points. It allows them to see the product in action, which can be more impactful than simply reading or hearing about it.
- ✓ Build Trust and Confidence: By offering a hands-on experience, product demos help build trust and confidence in the product and the sales professional. Customers can see the product's performance and features firsthand, leading to increased trust in its ability to deliver the promised results.
- ✓ Personalized Experience: Product demos can be tailored to each customer's unique

requirements and challenges. Sales professionals can focus on showcasing the features and benefits that are most relevant to the customer's specific needs, increasing the perceived value of the product.

- ✓ Overcoming Objections: Product demos provide an opportunity to address customer objections or concerns directly. Sales professionals can proactively demonstrate how the product addresses common pain points and resolves any potential issues, helping to overcome resistance and objections.
- ✓ Differentiation: In a competitive market, product demos can help differentiate your offering from competitors. By highlighting the unique features, capabilities, and benefits of your product, you can showcase why it stands out and why it is the best solution for the customer's needs.
- ✓ Speed up Decision-Making: Product demos can expedite the decision-making process. Seeing the product in action can help customers visualize how it will fit into their workflow and how it can improve their operations. It provides a tangible demonstration of the value proposition, making it easier for customers to make informed decisions.
- ✓ Increased Sales Conversion: Well-executed product demos have the potential to significantly increase sales conversion rates. By effectively showcasing the product's value and addressing customer needs, demos can

create a sense of urgency and motivate customers to move forward with the purchase.

- ✓ Customer Engagement and Satisfaction: Product demos offer a highly engaging and interactive experience for customers. It allows them to actively participate, ask questions, and provide feedback. This level of engagement leads to higher customer satisfaction and a stronger relationship between the sales professional and the customer.
- ✓ Knowledge Transfer: Product demos facilitate knowledge transfer by providing customers with a deeper understanding of the product. They can learn how to use the product effectively, which reduces the learning curve and ensures a smooth implementation process.

As seen, product demos are a powerful tool in technical sales that can effectively communicate the value and benefits of a product. They enhance customer understanding, build trust, overcome objections, and accelerate the decision-making process, ultimately leading to increased sales and customer satisfaction.

Steps to providing Product Demos

When providing a product demo to a technical sales customer, it is essential to follow a structured approach that effectively showcases the features, functionality, and value of your product. Here are the steps involved in providing a product demo to a technical sales customer:

- ✓ Understand Customer Needs: Before the demo, gather information about the customer's specific requirements, pain points, and desired outcomes. This understanding will help you tailor the demo to their needs and highlight relevant features and benefits.

- ✓ Set Objectives: Determine the objectives of the demo, whether it is to address specific pain points, showcase key features, or demonstrate the product's competitive advantage. Having clear objectives will help you stay focused during the demo.
- ✓ Plan the Demo Flow: Structure the demo in a logical and organized manner. Start with a brief introduction and agenda, and then proceed to demonstrate the key features, functionality, and benefits of the product. Consider the customer's specific needs and customize the demo accordingly.
- ✓ Highlight Key Features and Benefits: Emphasize the features and benefits that are most relevant to the customer. Explain how these features address their pain points and provide value to their business. Use real-life examples or case studies to illustrate the impact of your product.
- ✓ Engage the Customer: Involve the customer during the demo by asking questions, seeking their feedback, and encouraging them to interact with the product. This engagement helps them visualize how the product can address their specific needs and increases their investment in the demo process.
- ✓ Address Technical Questions: Be prepared to handle technical questions or concerns during the demo. Demonstrate your expertise by providing detailed explanations, technical specifications, or offering to connect them with

a technical expert if needed. Address any doubts or uncertainties to instill confidence in the product.

- ✓ Show Use Cases: If possible, showcase practical use cases or scenarios that align with the customer's industry or business needs. This demonstrates the product's applicability and helps the customer envision how it can solve their specific challenges.
- ✓ Tailor the Demo: Customize the demo to the customer's technical proficiency. Adapt your language and level of technical detail to ensure they understand and appreciate the product's capabilities without overwhelming them with unnecessary complexity.
- ✓ Recap and Summarize: After the demo, summarize the key points, features, and benefits covered during the session. Reinforce how the product can address the customer's needs and offer a solution to their pain points.
- ✓ Seek Feedback and Next Steps: Ask for feedback from the customer to gauge their level of interest and address any remaining questions or concerns. Based on their response, discuss the next steps, such as scheduling a follow-up meeting, providing additional materials, or initiating the sales process.

Remember, a successful product demo not only showcases the technical aspects of your product but also addresses the customer's specific needs and demonstrates the value it brings to their business. By following these steps, you can effectively engage technical sales customers and increase the likelihood of closing a successful deal.

Here are a Few Examples of Technical Demos

Example 1: Software Solution Demo for a Manufacturing Company

Step 1: Introduction and Agenda

- ✓ Introduce yourself and establish rapport with the customer.
- ✓ Briefly explain the agenda of the demo, including the key features and benefits that will be covered.

Step 2: Understand Customer Needs

- ✓ Ask the customer about their specific pain points and challenges in their manufacturing processes.
- ✓ Gather information on their requirements and goals for implementing a software solution.

Step 3: Highlight Key Features

- ✓ Demonstrate the software's user-friendly interface and intuitive navigation.
- ✓ Showcase features such as inventory management, production scheduling, and real-time analytics.
- ✓ Emphasize how these features streamline operations, reduce costs, and improve overall efficiency.

Step 4: Customization and Integration

- ✓ Illustrate the software's flexibility by showcasing the ability to customize workflows and reports to align with the customer's unique requirements.
- ✓ Discuss integration capabilities with existing systems, such as ERP or MES, to ensure a seamless transition.

Step 5: Real-Time Analytics and Reporting

- ✓ Showcase the software's robust reporting capabilities, including customizable dashboards and data visualization tools.
- ✓ Demonstrate how the customer can gain actionable insights into production performance, quality control, and resource optimization.

Step 6: Use Case Scenarios

- ✓ Share real-life examples of how similar manufacturing companies have successfully implemented the software and achieved significant improvements in productivity and profitability.
- ✓ Provide case studies or testimonials to reinforce the benefits and ROI of the solution.

Step 7: Address Technical Questions

- ✓ Encourage the customer to ask technical questions or raise concerns.
- ✓ Provide detailed explanations, address integration compatibility, data security, and scalability.
- ✓ Offer to connect the customer with technical experts for more in-depth discussions, if required.

Step 8: Recap and Next Steps

- ✓ Summarize the key features and benefits covered during the demo.
- ✓ Confirm the customer's interest and address any remaining questions or concerns.
- ✓ Discuss the next steps, such as a trial period, a follow-up meeting, or initiating the sales process.

Example 2: Hardware Equipment Demo for a Construction Company

Step 1: Introduction and Purpose

- ✓ Introduce yourself and your company, establishing credibility and expertise in the construction industry.
- ✓ Explain the purpose of the demo, focusing on how the equipment can address the customer's specific construction needs.

Step 2: Customer Requirements and Challenges

- ✓ Ask the customer about their ongoing construction projects and the challenges they face.
- ✓ Understand their specific requirements in terms of efficiency, safety, and productivity.

Step 3: Equipment Features and Benefits

- ✓ Demonstrate the key features of the equipment, such as durability, precision, and ease of use.
- ✓ Highlight how these features directly address the customer's pain points and improve construction processes.

Step 4: Operational Efficiency and Safety

- ✓ Showcase how the equipment enhances operational efficiency, reduces downtime, and increases productivity.
- ✓ Emphasize safety features and certifications that ensure compliance with industry regulations.

Step 5: Hands-On Demonstration

- ✓ Provide a hands-on experience for the customer, allowing them to operate the equipment or observe a live demonstration.
- ✓ Explain the steps involved in setting up, operating, and maintaining the equipment.

Step 6: Cost and ROI Analysis

- ✓ Discuss the cost-effectiveness and long-term return on investment of the equipment.
- ✓ Highlight potential cost savings, increased project efficiency, and reduced labour requirements.

Step 7: Customer Testimonials and Success Stories

- ✓ Share testimonials or case studies from other construction companies that have successfully implemented the equipment.
- ✓ Provide concrete examples of how the equipment has improved project outcomes and generated positive results.

Step 8: Addressing Concerns and Questions

- ✓ Encourage the customer to raise any concerns or questions they may have.
- ✓ Provide clear and detailed answers, addressing technical specifications, maintenance requirements, and warranty information.

Step 9: Recap and Next Steps

- ✓ Summarize the key points covered during the demo, focusing on the benefits that align with the customer's needs.
- ✓ Confirm the customer's interest and address any remaining questions or concerns.
- ✓ Discuss the next steps, such as providing a detailed quote, arranging a site visit, or initiating the purchasing process.

Example 3: Technical Instrument Demo for a Research Laboratory

Step 1: Introduction and Background

- ✓ Introduce yourself and your company, emphasizing your expertise in providing technical instruments for research laboratories.
- ✓ Briefly explain the purpose of the demo and how the instrument can contribute to the customer's research goals.

Step 2: Understanding Research Objectives

- ✓ Engage in a discussion with the customer to understand their specific research objectives, challenges, and desired outcomes.
- ✓ Gather information about their experimental techniques and the parameters they need to measure.

Step 3: Instrument Features and Specifications

- ✓ Demonstrate the key features of the instrument, focusing on its accuracy, precision, and reliability.
- ✓ Explain the technical specifications that make it suitable for the customer's research requirements.

Step 4: Experimental Setup and Data Collection

- ✓ Showcase how the instrument can be set up for the customer's specific experiments or measurements.
- ✓ Provide a step-by-step demonstration of how to collect accurate data using the instrument.

Step 5: Data Analysis and Interpretation

- ✓ Illustrate how the instrument's software or data analysis tools can help analyze and interpret the collected data.

- ✓ Showcase features such as data visualization, statistical analysis, and exporting capabilities.

Step 6: Calibration and Maintenance

- ✓ Explain the instrument's calibration process and maintenance requirements to ensure accurate and reliable measurements.
- ✓ Provide guidelines on how frequently the instrument needs calibration and the necessary maintenance procedures.

Step 7: Validation and Compliance

- ✓ Discuss any certifications or compliance standards relevant to the instrument, ensuring it meets the customer's regulatory requirements.
- ✓ Provide documentation or references to support the instrument's validation in similar research settings.

Step 8: Addressing Technical Questions

- ✓ Encourage the customer to ask technical questions related to the instrument's capabilities, compatibility, or limitations.
- ✓ Provide detailed and accurate answers, drawing on your technical expertise and product knowledge.

Step 9: Summary and Next Steps

- ✓ Summarize the key benefits of the instrument that align with the customer's research objectives.
- ✓ Seek feedback from the customer and address any remaining concerns or questions.
- ✓ Discuss the next steps, such as providing a formal quote, offering a trial period, or initiating the purchasing process.

By following a structured approach and customizing the demo to the customer's needs, you can effectively showcase the value and capabilities of your products or solutions.

Adding Personal Value

In sales, adding personal value is about going above and beyond to meet the needs and expectations of customers. This involves leveraging your expertise, providing exceptional support, and offering creative problem-solving solutions. By adding personal value, sales professionals can build stronger relationships with customers, differentiate themselves from competitors, and ultimately, drive more sales.

Ways You Can Personally Add Value

There are several ways that sales professionals can personally add value to their interactions with customers. Some examples include:

- ✓ Expertise: Sales professionals can add value by leveraging their expertise and knowledge to provide customers with valuable insights and advice. For example, a salesperson selling software might offer tips on how to optimize the software for maximum efficiency.
- ✓ Support: Providing exceptional support is another way to add value. This could involve helping customers navigate complex purchasing decisions, providing ongoing assistance after the sale, or offering training and education on how to use the product or service effectively.
- ✓ Problem-solving: Sales professionals can add value by offering creative problem-solving solutions to customers. This could involve identifying and addressing potential challenges or finding innovative ways to meet the customer's needs.

- ✓ Personalization: Personalizing the sales experience for customers can also add value. This could involve tailoring your approach to meet the specific needs and preferences of each customer or offering personalized recommendations based on their unique situation.
- ✓ Going the extra mile: Sometimes, adding value is as simple as going the extra mile to exceed customer expectations. This could involve offering additional services or benefits that are not typically included, such as free shipping or extended warranties.

Examples

An example of a sales professional adding personal value is a real estate agent who goes beyond simply showing houses to offering advice on neighborhoods, schools, and local amenities. By leveraging their expertise and providing exceptional support, the agent adds value to the customer's home-buying experience.

Another example is a salesperson selling software who provides personalized training and support to help customers get the most out of the product. By going the extra mile to ensure that customers are able to use the software effectively, the salesperson adds value and builds customer loyalty.

Action Plan & Strategies

To add personal value in sales, sales professionals can follow these action plans and strategies:

- ✓ Understand your customers: Take the time to understand your customers' needs, preferences, and challenges. This will help you tailor your approach and add value in a way that resonates with them.

- ✓ Leverage your expertise: Use your expertise and knowledge to provide customers with valuable insights and advice. This could involve offering tips, recommendations, or best practices that can help them achieve their goals.
- ✓ Provide exceptional support: Offer exceptional support before, during, and after the sale. This could involve being responsive to customer inquiries, providing timely assistance, and going above and beyond to meet customer needs.
- ✓ Offer creative problem-solving solutions: Be proactive in identifying and addressing potential challenges or issues that customers may face. Offer creative solutions that demonstrate your commitment to adding value.
- ✓ Personalize the sales experience: Tailor your approach to meet the specific needs and preferences of each customer. Offer personalized recommendations and solutions that are relevant to their unique situation.

By following these strategies, sales professionals can add personal value to their interactions with customers, differentiate themselves from competitors, and build stronger, more meaningful relationships that lead to increased sales and customer loyalty.

Other Ways to Add Value

In addition to expertise, support, problem-solving, and personalization, there are several other ways that sales professionals can add value to their interactions with customers. These additional strategies can help differentiate your offering, build stronger relationships, and drive more sales.

1. Build Trust: Building trust is essential in sales. Sales professionals can add value by being honest, transparent, and reliable in their interactions with customers. By demonstrating integrity and building trust, sales professionals can create a strong foundation for long-term relationships.
2. Provide Education: Providing education to customers can add value by helping them make informed decisions. This could involve offering resources such as whitepapers, case studies, or webinars that provide valuable insights and information relevant to the customer's needs.
3. Offer Customization: Offering customization options can add value by allowing customers to tailor your offering to meet their specific needs. This could involve offering different product configurations, pricing plans, or service levels to accommodate varying customer requirements.
4. Deliver Exceptional Service: Providing exceptional service can add value by exceeding customer expectations. This could involve offering fast response times, proactive

communication, and a high level of attention to detail in all interactions with customers.

5. Show Appreciation: Showing appreciation to customers can add value by making them feel valued and respected. This could involve sending thank-you notes, offering exclusive discounts or promotions, or providing special rewards for loyal customers.
6. Focus on Long-Term Relationships: Rather than focusing solely on making a sale, sales professionals can add value by focusing on building long-term relationships with customers. This involves taking the time to understand their needs and priorities and providing ongoing support and assistance even after the sale is made.

Examples

An example of a company that adds value by focusing on trust is Zappos, an online shoe and clothing retailer. Zappos is known for its exceptional customer service and commitment to building trust with its customers. By offering free shipping and returns, as well as a 365-day return policy, Zappos has built a loyal customer base that trusts the company to deliver a positive shopping experience.

Another example is Amazon, which adds value by offering a wide range of products and services, fast delivery options, and a seamless shopping experience. By focusing on customer satisfaction and convenience, Amazon has become a trusted and reliable source for millions of customers around the world.

Action Plan & Strategies

To incorporate these additional ways of adding value into their sales approach, sales professionals can follow these action plans and strategies:

- ✓ Identify Customer Needs: Take the time to understand your customers' needs, preferences, and challenges. This will help you identify opportunities to add value in meaningful ways.
- ✓ Tailor Your Approach: Tailor your approach to each customer based on their unique needs and preferences. Offer solutions that are relevant and valuable to them.
- ✓ Provide Ongoing Support: Offer ongoing support and assistance to customers even after the sale is made. This could involve offering training, troubleshooting assistance, or regular check-ins to ensure customer satisfaction.
- ✓ Seek Feedback: Regularly seek feedback from customers to understand how you can improve your offerings and better meet their needs. Use this feedback to make improvements and continue adding value.
- ✓ Stay Engaged: Stay engaged with customers through regular communication and updates. Keep them informed about new products, services, or promotions that may be of interest to them.

By incorporating these strategies into their sales approach, sales professionals can add value in a variety of ways that go beyond just the product or service itself. This can help build stronger relationships with customers, drive more sales, and ultimately, lead to greater success in sales.

After-Sales-Service: Powerful Strategies to Retain Customers for Life

Many Sales People today think that Customer Service is different from Sales. While this may be so, we must remind ourselves that every single person in the organization from the topmost person right to the lowest in rank can effect or have an impact on customers, by the way they treat them and therefore must have the *'hat'* of a Customer Service Professional too.

No business, especially during these downtimes can afford to ignore two very important people- **2C's** - **Your Customer** and **Your Competitor**! The person in front of you is your Customer, and if this person is not treated well, then the person behind you (Your Competitor!) is just waiting to grab him as he drops from your list!

Retaining existing customers especially during a downtime could be tough, as it is in these tough times, it is even more difficult, though, important to listen to your existing customers, understand their problems, offer them insightful support, and do everything you can to help them survive. But there is a payoff for retaining customers: it is less costly than acquiring new customers. It costs six times more to acquire a new customer than it does to keep an existing customer.

So what then is this **Customer Service or Experience**?

Customer Service or their Experience is the customers' perception of how your company treats them. These perceptions affect their behaviors and build memories and feelings that will drive their loyalty. In other words: if they like you and continue to like you, they are going to do business with you and recommend you to others.

And for your customers to like you, you should know them very well to create and deliver personalized experiences that will entice their loyalty. But gaining this in-depth knowledge about customers isn't something that just happens. You as the Sales Person will need to work on this with your Customer. No doubt, this is well worth the effort.

And it doesn't matter what kind of business you are in – improving the experience for your customers is the key to increasing retention, satisfaction and sales.

Here are some vital data that can help you look at this area of your job on priority

1. *For consumers, customer experience will become more important than price and product in the future.*
2. *89% of businesses compete through the level of customer experience they're able to deliver.* -Gartner
3. *70% of the customer's journey is dictated by how the customer feels they are being treated.* -McKinsey
4. *Businesses that deliver better customer experiences obtain revenues between 4% and 8% above their market.* -Bain & Company
5. *55% of customers are willing to spend more money with a company that guarantees them a satisfying experience.* –Think Jar
6. *70% of unhappy customers whose problems are resolved are willing to shop with a business again.* - Glance
7. *Customer service stats show that new customers cost anywhere between 5 and 25 times more than*

retaining existing customers. -Harvard Business Review
8. *44% of consumers take their business elsewhere due to a poor experience.* –NewVoiceMedia
9. *50% of customers switch brands when their needs are not met.*
10. *13% of customers tell 15 people or more if they have a negative experience.* - Esteban Kolsky
11. *After one negative experience, 51% of customers will never do business with that company again.* - NewVoiceMedia
12. *72% of customers will tell 6 people or more if they have a satisfying experience*. - Esteban Kolsky
13. *67% of customers report a bad customer experience as the reason for switching businesses.* - Esteban Kolsky
14. Only 1 in 26 customers will tell a business about their negative experience; the rest simply leave according to customer service facts. -Esteban Kolsky
15. 79% of customers who share their complaints online see their complaints ignored. -RightNow

Customers usually don't care about what good you do! On an average when a customer is happy with a product or service, they would generally tell around 7 people, but if the service was bad or if they were disappointed with it, guess how many they would tell on an average?
Without considering the internet, the answer is 38 (just lip service)! But today, with almost everyone in possession of a mobile phone having an internet connection, you do not have to guess the figure! Bad News certainly travels faster than Good News! You don't have to look far...See today's newspaper headlines, or turn to any news channel or get onto

any social media site...What do you get more of? Good news or bad news?

Word-of-mouth advertising is the most powerful form of advertising in the world. And this is what you as a Professional need to keep in mind!

Remember- there are only 3 entrances to any business....

- ✓ *The Front Door!*
- ✓ *The Telephone!*
- ✓ *The Internet!*

...And if either of these are NOT handled well, you have LOST your Customer forever!

And in some businesses, this figure can be very high.

And remember women are great INFLUENCERS!

A survey carried out on **"Why customers quit"** found the following:

- ✓ *3% move away*
- ✓ *5% develop other friendships*
- ✓ *9% leave for competitive reasons*
- ✓ *14% are dissatisfied with the product*
- ✓ *68% quit* ***because of an attitude*** *of indifference toward the customer by the owner, manager or some employee.*

(With the total showing 99%, you could be wondering what happened to that 1%- Well, because of the death of some of them!)

If you do a little calculation, you will find that a good over 90% is well within your control of turning this around as a Sales Professional.

Studies show that increasing customer retention rates by just 5% will increase profits anywhere from 25% to 95%, depending on the business you are in.

And remember that your customers won't love you if you give poor service, but your competitors will certainly love you!

Every time a Customer complains try looking at the **'Complaint as a Gift'!**

Unfortunately, what often happens is that the front line employees who receive complaints take them personally or blame others. As a result, they over-react and become defensive.

To overcome this kind of reaction, it can help to think of the complaint as a genuine desire to solve the problem by someone who has taken the time and the trouble to visit, write or telephone.

A chance to set things right! And probably, the <u>only</u> chance!

How many times you would have experienced that all that the customer really wanted when he complained was an acknowledgement of the problem, an apology, an explanation and a solution to the problem. And the solution offered could have been just a refund, a replacement, an upgrade or just a hearing!

By complaining, customers are giving you several opportunities like:

- ✓ Helping you find out what you need to do to improve your systems and procedures
- ✓ See your service from the customer's point of view and try to make changes- He is the spokesperson for the many others that do not open up.
- ✓ Identify areas where your company could train your staff.
- ✓ Help you identify new products/ services/ opportunities which the market may require from you. (This is free information that you can get!)

- ✓ When customers share their story, they're not just sharing pain points. They're actually teaching you how to make your product, service, and business better.

So it is important to know what your Customers want!

All callers want **C.A.S.H.**

- ✓ **C**onvenience (at theirs, not yours!)
- ✓ **A**ction (not just lip service!)
- ✓ **S**peed (Everyone wants an answer immediately/ early/ now!)
- ✓ **H**assle-free (Not being shunted from one department to another!)

Among B2B decision makers, lack of speed in interactions with their suppliers is the number one pain point, mentioned twice as often as price.

When it comes to making a purchase, 64% of people find customer experience more important than price.

So what are some of the Pre-requisites for handling complaints?

- ✓ Top Management to have the 'Right Attitude' (as this attitude very soon percolates down-knowing what is done, is what the organization rewards)
- ✓ The 'Right Attitude' and behaviour of people receiving the complaints
- ✓ Strong Systems, Policies and Procedures (Not just Smiles!)

There are eight main stages to Handling Complaints:

1. Listen and stay calm: Aim to diffuse the customer's feelings and clarify the exact nature of the problem.

2. Sympathize: This means sympathizing with the fact that the person has a problem, not accepting any

blame (as you yet have not heard both sides of the case).
3. Don't justify, argue, make excuses, interrupt or pass the buck: Just stick to the facts, keep off what happened in the past and focus on what is going to happen now.
4. Ask probing questions to verify facts: This will give you more detailed information about the specific complaint and allow you to see a way through to a possible solution to the problem
5. Check back your understanding: Reconfirm or paraphrase what you heard.
6. Agree a course of action and timeframe: It is essential to find a solution which is satisfactory for the customer and from your organization's point of view.
7. Thank them
8. Check the course of action is carried out: If you agree with the customer that something will happen by a certain date, you must check that it has in fact happened. If it hasn't, you must take action to avoid making the problem even more serious.

The Things That Customers Want!

Various researches have identified a number of factors that seem to influence customers' decision to remain loyal.

- ✓ *You keep your promises*
- ✓ *You are willing to help*
- ✓ *You inspire confidence*
- ✓ *You treat customers as individuals*
- ✓ *You make it easy for customers to do business with you.*
- ✓ *All the physical aspects of your product or service give a favorable impression.*

In Closing, let me just give you the Key that is summed up in one word: **C.A.R.E:**

Customers

Are

Really

Everything!

Measuring Success

Measuring the success of your sales efforts is crucial for evaluating the effectiveness of your strategies and identifying areas for improvement. This chapter explores strategies for measuring success in terms of customer satisfaction, retention, and revenue growth, including examples and action plans:

1. **Defining Success Metrics**: Identify key performance indicators (KPIs) that align with your sales goals, such as customer satisfaction scores, customer retention rates, and revenue growth targets.
   Example: A software company defines success metrics that include customer satisfaction ratings, customer retention rates, and monthly recurring revenue (MRR) growth.
2. **Implementing Tracking Systems**: Use customer relationship management (CRM) systems and other tracking tools to monitor and analyze sales performance against your defined KPIs.
   Example: A retail store uses a CRM system to track customer purchases, analyze trends, and identify opportunities for up-selling and cross-selling.
3. **Collecting Customer Feedback**: Gather feedback from customers through surveys, reviews, and direct communication to gauge their satisfaction with your products or services.
   Example: A hotel collects feedback from guests through post-stay surveys and online

reviews to understand their experience and improve service quality.

4. **Analyzing Sales Data**: Analyze sales data to identify trends, patterns, and areas for improvement. Use this information to adjust your sales strategies and tactics accordingly.
   Example: A car dealership analyzes sales data to identify the most popular models and features, adjusting inventory and marketing efforts accordingly.
5. **Setting Realistic Goals**: Set realistic and achievable sales goals based on your historical data and market trends. Regularly review and adjust these goals as needed.
   Example: A software company sets a goal to increase customer satisfaction ratings by 10% within the next year, based on current performance and industry benchmarks.
6. **Tracking Customer Retention**: Monitor customer retention rates to understand how well you are retaining existing customers and identify opportunities to improve loyalty.
   Example: A subscription-based service tracks its customer churn rate to identify reasons for customer attrition and implement strategies to reduce churn.
7. **Measuring Revenue Growth**: Track revenue growth over time to assess the effectiveness of your sales efforts and identify areas for revenue optimization.
   Example: A consulting firm tracks its monthly revenue growth to evaluate the impact of new client acquisitions and service offerings.

Action Plan:

- ✓ Goal Setting Workshop: Conduct a workshop to set specific, measurable, achievable, relevant, and time-bound (SMART) goals for your sales team.
- ✓ CRM Training: Provide training on how to use your CRM system effectively to track and analyze sales data.
- ✓ Customer Feedback Surveys: Implement regular customer feedback surveys to gather insights into customer satisfaction and identify areas for improvement.
- ✓ Sales Performance Reviews: Conduct regular reviews of sales performance against KPIs to identify top performers and areas for improvement.
- ✓ Continuous Improvement: Encourage a culture of continuous improvement within your sales team, where feedback and learnings are shared and used to refine sales strategies.

By implementing these strategies and action plans, you can effectively measure the success of your sales efforts in terms of customer satisfaction, retention, and revenue growth, and make informed decisions to drive sales performance.

Conclusion

In **"The Power of Value Selling:** *A Guide to Selling from the Customer's Perspective,"* we have explored the key principles of value selling and how they can be applied to enhance your sales effectiveness. Throughout this book, we have emphasized the importance of understanding customer needs, positioning your offering as a solution to those needs, and demonstrating the value of your product or service.

As you conclude your journey through this book, it is important to reflect on the key learnings and takeaways:

1. **Customer-Centric Approach**: Always prioritize the customer's needs and interests. By understanding their challenges and goals, you can tailor your approach to provide maximum value.
2. **Selling Value, Not Price**: Shift your focus from competing on price to highlighting the unique value proposition of your offering. Customers are willing to pay more for products or services that provide greater value and benefits.
3. **Building Trust and Credibility**: Honesty, transparency, and delivering on promises are key to building trust with customers. Trust is the foundation of long-lasting relationships and repeat business.
4. **Ethical Selling Practices**: Uphold ethical standards in your sales interactions. Respect customer boundaries and avoid manipulative tactics that could damage your reputation.

5. **Negotiation for Win-Win Outcomes**: Use negotiation techniques to achieve win-win outcomes that provide value for both you and the customer. Focus on creating mutually beneficial agreements.
6. **Upselling and Cross-selling Opportunities**: Identify opportunities to upsell or cross-sell by understanding the customer's broader needs and offering complementary products or services.

Action Plan:

- ✓ Implement Value Selling Techniques: Begin by incorporating the value selling techniques outlined in this book into your sales process. Focus on understanding customer needs, highlighting value, and building trust.
- ✓ Continuous Learning and Improvement: Sales is an ever-evolving field. Stay updated with industry trends and best practices. Attend training programs and seek feedback to continuously improve your skills.
- ✓ Customer Feedback and Engagement: Regularly collect feedback from customers to understand their satisfaction levels and areas for improvement. Engage with customers through surveys, reviews, and direct communication.
- ✓ Set Clear Goals and Metrics: Define clear sales goals and metrics to track your progress. Regularly review your performance against these metrics and adjust your strategies as needed.
- ✓ Collaborate with Marketing and Product Teams: Work closely with your marketing and

product teams to align your sales efforts with the overall business goals. Share insights and feedback to drive product improvements and marketing strategies.

- ✓ By adopting a customer-centric approach, focusing on value, and continuously improving your sales skills, you can achieve greater success in your sales career.

Thank you for joining us on this journey, and we wish you all the best in your future sales endeavors.

About the Author
'GERARD ASSEY'

Gerard Assey is a Graduate in Economics, a PGD in Management (HRD) and holds a Doctorate in Leadership. Gerard holds several International Qualifications in Sales, Debt Collection, Training & Teaching, and is a 'Fellow' of the prestigious 'Institute of Sales & Marketing Management'-UK, a Certified NLP Practitioner, a 'Certified Trainer', an 'Accredited Management Teacher-Behavioral Sciences', a 'Certified Competency Facilitator', a 'Certified Management Consultant'- (the International credentials of a professional management consultant, awarded in accordance with global standards of the ICMCI); and a Certification from the University of Michigan in 'Successful Negotiation: Essential Strategies and Skills'

He is also a Member of the 'National Association of Sales Professionals' backed with several years experience in varied industries, both in India and Overseas. He also holds an 'Etiquette Consultant' Certification from the USA (by Sue Fox, Author of Best Seller: 'Business Etiquette for Dummies'. She has trained some of the top celebrities' world over). He was also a recipient of a scholarship for extensive training in Japan on 'Corporate Management for India'.

Gerard Assey is 'Founder & Chief Corporate Trainer' of the Group: '**Citius, Altius, Fortius Unlimited**'- an organization that **celebrated 20 years of Glorious Service** in 2021, focusing on 3 Core Competencies:

People. Performance. Profit; in functional areas of Sales & Marketing, HR & Organizational Development, covering Recruitment, Training & Consultancy!

Having managed organizations with large Sales Forces in India & Overseas, his specialization cover extensive areas of Sales Training (All levels - Presentation, Negotiation, Key/ Strategic Accounts Management & Managerial Skills for all sectors), Bid Proposal/ Capture Planning/ Management Trainings, Retail Sales, Customer Service & Customer Retention Programs, Training for Prevention & Collection of Debt, Self & Personal Development Programs (Time Management, Teamwork & Team Building, Business Etiquette & Personal Grooming, Leadership & Managerial Skills, People Management Skills, Train-the-Trainer etc), including preparation of Custom-designed Business Manuals for Internal (HR, Induction, and Sales etc) & External use (Instruction, User Manuals).

Gerard has successfully conducted over 6080 Trainings & Workshops (as of Feb '24) all across India, Middle East, Africa, Europe & S.E. Asia. Besides public programs conducted regularly, both in India & Overseas, he has some of the top names as clients whom he services from Single Owners to large Public & Government undertakings, covering all sectors, for their in-house needs.

His website: www.CollectionSkills.com is the only one in this part of the world to be featured in the 'Collections & Credit Risk Magazine-USA' under 'Who's Who in Training' and ranks TOP, along with other websites listed below on most search engines.

Gerard is author of 113 books already (Mar 2024)

A few of our business related books:

1. Bite-sized Bits on Commonsense Management
2. Heart to Heart on Life's Principles'
3. How to become a Successful Manager
4. The Sales Professionals' Master Workbook of S.Y.S.T.E.M.S
5. The Professional Business Email Etiquette Handbook & Guide
6. The Professional Business Video-Conferencing Etiquette Handbook & Guide
7. Professional Presentation Skills
8. Exceptional Customer Service
9. Professional Tele-Marketing Skills
10. Professional Debt Collection Skills
11. The G.R.E.A.T. Sales & Service Workbook
12. Sales Training Advantage for Results (*The Ultimate Sales Training Manual to enable you stand out as a S.T.A.R.*)
13. CEO Daily Planner & Organizer
14. The Sales Professionals' Master Daily Planner
15. The Professional Debt Collector's Master Daily Planner
16. My Daily Planner & Organizer
17. MY EMERGENCY INFORMATION RECORD (Family Emergency & Peace of Mind Planner)
18. The Ultimate Therapist & Counselors Planner and Organizer
19. Building an Ethical Workplace
20. Managing Relationships at Work
21. Managing Business Meetings Effectively
22. Effective Delegation Skills
23. Goal Setting for Success
24. B2B Selling by Email
25. Professional Business Etiquette & Grooming
26. Dining Etiquette & Table Manners
27. Effective Networking Skills
28. Grooming, Etiquette & Manners for Teens, Young Adults & Future Leaders
29. Inter-Personal Skills
30. Get Ready, Get Hired!
31. Selling in a Recession
32. Effective Receivables Management in an Economic Downturn!
33. Real Estate & Property Sales Training

34. Credit Sales & Accounts Receivable Management
35. Selling Skills for Real Estate & Property Advisors
36. Take G.R.E.A.T. C.A.R.E!
37. Spa, Salon & Health Club Selling Skills
38. Selling Travel, Holiday & MICE Services
39. Selling Skills for Spa's, Salons & Health Clubs
40. Retailing in Salons & Spas
41. Selling Holiday, Vacation, Tours & Packages
42. The Power of Sales Referrals
43. Selling Luxury
44. Technical Selling Skills
45. Financial Advisors Sales Training
46. Dealing with Burnout at Work Monopolize Your Markets
47. Selling to Affluent Customers
48. Growing up with Grace
49. Financial Selling Skills
50. *The Effective Manager's Guide: Key Skills to Thrive*
51. From Aspiring to Inspiring: A Guide for New Managers on the Rise
52. The Power of Focus
53. Selling with Integrity: Sell Like Jesus The Perfect Role Model!
54. 31 Habits of Champions: Your 31-Day Journey to Greatness
55. Rejecting Grasshopper Talk: From Grasshopper to Giant-Killer-*Defeating Giants Daily!*
56. Navigate the AI-Powered Future of Bid & Proposals: Up-Skill to Stay Relevant with Alternative Career Paths & Opportunities
57. Hiring Sales Winners
58. Present with Impact
59. Success Unlocked: *Breaking Free from Habits that Hold You Back*
60. Complaints to Cheers, Feedback to Gold: Mastering Complaints Management
61. Thriving Together: *Cultivating Diversity, Equity, and Inclusion*
62. Coaching Skills for Sales Managers
63. Soaring to Success in Business & Leadership: Swifter, Higher, Stronger!
64. From Classroom to Podium: A Student's Guide to Powerful Public Speaking & Presentation Skills

65. Developing Self-Discipline
66. The CEO's 31-Day Power Plan: Unlocking Success through Essential Traits
67. Credibility Matters
68. A Winning Attitude
69. Bid & Proposal Management Using AI
70. Sales Forecasting: A Practical & Proven Guide to Strategic Sales Forecasting
71. Elevate & Energize: *50 Dynamic & Fun Activities for Peak Workplace Morale*
72. 'Sales SOS! Sales on Fire! *30 Days to Conquer Chaos & the Nightmares of Success!'*
73. Mastering Sales Managerial Skills: *Building High-Performing Teams & Driving Exceptional Results*
74. Eagle-Eyed Leadership: Unleashing the Power of 31 Lessons from Eagles
75. The Ultimate Employee Training Guide: *Training Today, Leading Tomorrow*
76. Being More Accountable at Work
77. Creating a Culture of Continuous Improvement
78. Effective Questioning & Listening Skills
79. The Power of Value Selling

Besides regularly contributing to business & trade journals, including international ones such as the 'Creative Training Techniques' and the 'Sales News' of the U.S.A, He is also a member of several prestigious bodies & trade associations, having participated in many Conferences & Workshops in India & Overseas.

Prior to his last assignment of leading & managing a large MNC as head, Gerard had a 3-year stint in the Middle East as a Consultant with a leading British Consultancy Firm.

As the past 'Official Country Representative' for the International Business Award- 'THE STEVIES'-(the business world's own Oscar) for about 4 years- he ensured a few Indian companies that qualify for the same every year!

Gerard can be contacted at:
Email: training@Sales-Training.in,training@CollectionSkills.com
Websites:

www.Sales-Training.in
www.EtiquetteWorks.in
www.CollectionSkills.com
www.RetailSalesTraining.in
www.SalesTrainingIndia.com
www.ManualPreparation.com
www.TrainingWithPuppets.com
www.FirstContactAcademy.com
www.SalesAndMarketingRecruiter.com

Our TRAININGS that can help your team

- ✓ **Sales Effectiveness**: Selling Skills for any Sector: Service/ Logistics/ FMCG Realty/ Insurance & Finance/ Media/ SPA's, Health Clubs & Salons/ Key Account Management, Effective Negotiation Skills/ Bid & Proposal Management Skills/ Retail Sales Training: Any Sector (Auto, Jewelry, Clothing, Luxury etc)
- ✓ **Customer Service Skills**-Complaints Handling & Customer Retention
- ✓ **Debt Prevention & Collection Skills**
- ✓ **Etiquette & Grooming**
- ✓ **Leadership & Managerial Skills**
- ✓ **Self & Personal Development Skills**: Presentation Skills/ Effective Communication Skills/Business Proposal Writing Skills/ Problem Solving & Decision Making Skills/ Empowering Secretaries-The perfect PA! (For Secretaries & PA's)/ Effective Time Management/ Teamwork & Teambuilding/ P.R.I.D.E- **P**ersonal **R**esponsibility **I**n **D**elivering **E**xcellence

www.ingramcontent.com/pod-product-compliance
Lightning Source LLC
LaVergne TN
LVHW010106170826
845678LV00012B/2261